Please note the information contained within this document is
for educational and entertainment purposes only. Every
attempt has been made to provide accurate, up to date and
reliable complete information. No warranties of any kind are
expressed or implied. Readers acknowledge that the author is
not engaging in the rendering of legal, financial, medical or
professional advice. The content of this book has been derived
from various sources. Please consult a licensed professional
before attempting any techniques outlined in this book.

By reading this document, the readers agree that under no
circumstances are the author responsible for any losses, direct
or indirect, which are incurred as a result of the use of
information contained within this document, including but not
limited to errors, omissions or inaccuracies.

Thank you very much for reading this book.

Title: Where Cross-Border Payments Fail: The Need for Ripple's XRP Ledger
Subtitle: Examining the Friction Facing Global Transfers

Series: Bridging Borders: XRP's Vision for Faster, Efficient Worldwide Transactions: Ripple's Mission to Revolutionize Payments through Blockchain Innovation
Author: Jonathan T. Morgan

Table of Contents

Introduction

Brief history of cross-border payments

Cross-border payments, the intricate web that intertwines global financial transactions, have a storied history shaped by the evolution of trade, technology, and the financial systems that underpin international commerce. As we embark on an exploration of the current state of cross-border payments and Ripple's vision for transformation using the XRP Ledger, it is essential to delve into the annals of time and understand the genesis of these intricate financial networks.

The Early Days of Cross-Border Transactions

The roots of cross-border payments can be traced back to the earliest forms of trade and commerce. In ancient times, barter systems dominated, and direct exchanges were prevalent. As societies evolved, so did the need for more sophisticated means of conducting transactions across borders. The advent of currencies, both physical and digital, marked a significant turning point.

In medieval Europe, bills of exchange emerged as a tool to facilitate trade between merchants in different regions. These were essentially promissory notes that could be traded, serving as a precursor to modern-day negotiable instruments. The rise of banking institutions during the Renaissance further streamlined cross-border transactions, allowing merchants to conduct business beyond their immediate geographic boundaries.

The Gold Standard Era

The 19th century saw the establishment of the gold standard, a monetary system where the value of a country's currency was directly linked to a specific quantity of gold. This standardized approach aimed to bring stability to international trade and finance. However, the gold standard had its limitations, and the interwar period witnessed its eventual collapse due to economic pressures and geopolitical turmoil.

Post-World War II: The Bretton Woods System

In the aftermath of World War II, the Bretton Woods Conference in 1944 laid the foundation for a new international monetary system. The resultant Bretton Woods Agreement established fixed exchange rates pegged to the U.S. dollar, which, in turn, was convertible to gold. This system facilitated a degree of stability, but it faced challenges as economic imbalances and inflationary pressures mounted.

The Rise of SWIFT and Correspondent Banking

The 1970s saw the establishment of the Society for Worldwide Interbank Financial Telecommunication (SWIFT), a cooperative messaging network designed to facilitate secure and standardized communication between financial institutions globally. SWIFT revolutionized the way banks communicated, but the underlying settlement mechanisms continued to rely on correspondent banking relationships. This model introduced delays, inefficiencies, and complexities into cross-border transactions.

Challenges in the 21st Century

As we progressed into the 21st century, technological advancements accelerated the pace of global trade, necessitating more agile and efficient cross-border payment systems. However, legacy systems struggled to keep up, leading to the persistence of pain points that hindered the seamless flow of funds across borders.

The Digital Revolution and the Need for Change

The rise of the internet and digital technologies heralded a new era for cross-border payments. The demand for faster, cheaper, and more transparent transactions became increasingly pronounced. However, the existing financial infrastructure, laden with intermediaries, regulatory hurdles, and outdated technology, proved to be a bottleneck in achieving these goals.

As we navigate through the historical currents of cross-border payments, it becomes evident that the need for a transformative solution has never been more urgent. In the following chapters, we will dissect the pain points ingrained in the current system, exploring the impediments to speed, the high costs associated with transactions, the challenges of access, and the overarching call for modernization. It is within this context that Ripple's XRP Ledger emerges as a potential catalyst for change, offering a vision for a future where cross-border payments align with the demands of our interconnected and rapidly evolving global economy.

Pain points with current systems

In the intricate tapestry of global finance, cross-border payments serve as the vital threads weaving together nations, businesses, and individuals. Yet, beneath the surface of this interconnected web, lies a landscape fraught with inefficiencies, delays, and complexities inherent in the current systems facilitating international transactions. This chapter peels back the layers to unveil the pain points that have long plagued cross-border payments, setting the stage for a critical examination of why change is not only necessary but imperative.

The Pervasive Challenge of Speed in International Transfers

One of the most glaring pain points in the current cross-border payment landscape is the lethargic pace at which funds move across borders. While domestic transactions have embraced real-time processing, the international counterpart remains trapped in a time warp of delays and uncertainties. The contrast between the instantaneous nature of local transfers and the sluggish pace of cross-border transactions is stark, impacting individuals and businesses alike.

Batch processing, a common practice in the current systems, introduces significant delays. Transactions often wait in queues until a predefined batch size is reached, leading to unnecessary lags in processing times. This antiquated approach is a remnant of legacy systems and contributes to the frustratingly slow experience users face when conducting international transfers.

The correspondent banking model, another cornerstone of the current cross-border payment infrastructure, exacerbates the issue of speed. The need for multiple intermediary banks to facilitate a single transaction introduces layers of complexity and bureaucracy. Each intermediary bank adds its own processing time, cumulatively elongating the end-to-end duration of a transaction.

The impact of delayed transfers reverberates through various sectors. Individuals relying on timely remittances for essential expenses, such as education or healthcare, find their plans disrupted. Businesses engaged in international trade face challenges in managing working capital and responding promptly to market dynamics. The current speed constraints are not merely inconveniences; they represent tangible barriers to economic growth and financial inclusion.

The Weight of Cost: Fees, Spreads, and Lack of Transparency

Beyond the issue of speed, the cost associated with cross-border payments poses a formidable challenge. Sending money across borders often incurs exorbitant fees, acting as a deterrent for individuals and businesses alike. The fees levied by intermediary banks for their services, coupled with currency conversion charges, can significantly erode the value of the transferred funds.

Foreign exchange spreads, the difference between the buying and selling prices of currencies, further contribute to the overall cost burden. The lack of transparency surrounding these spreads adds an additional layer of frustration for users, who are left in the dark about the true cost of their transactions. This opacity in fee structures hinders users from making informed decisions and planning their financial activities effectively.

High transaction costs associated with cross-border payments have profound implications. Small and medium-sized enterprises (SMEs), often operating on tight budgets, face a disproportionate impact. For individuals in economically vulnerable regions, the cost of sending or receiving funds becomes a barrier to accessing essential services. The current fee structures, bereft of transparency and laden with unnecessary expenses, are a formidable obstacle to the democratization of cross-border transactions.

Access Denied: Challenges for the Unbanked and Emerging Markets

While the interconnected nature of global finance has facilitated unprecedented economic growth, a significant portion of the global population remains excluded from the formal financial system. Billions of individuals, predominantly in developing regions, find themselves on the fringes of financial services, facing barriers to entry that hinder their ability to participate in cross-border transactions.

The unbanked, lacking access to traditional banking services, are excluded from the benefits of cross-border transactions. This exclusion exacerbates existing inequalities, hindering economic development and perpetuating financial disparities. Emerging markets, despite their potential for growth, face friction in integrating with the global financial system, limiting their ability to participate fully in international trade and commerce.

Small businesses operating in these regions encounter substantial challenges when attempting to access cross-border payment systems. The complex procedures, stringent requirements, and lack of tailored solutions for smaller enterprises act as deterrents. As a result, these businesses find themselves at a disadvantage, unable to harness the full potential of global markets.

The Opacity Quandary: Limited Visibility and Tracking

Transparency, a fundamental pillar of trust in any financial system, is notably lacking in current cross-border payment mechanisms. Participants in the payment chain often experience limited visibility into the status and location of their funds during the transfer process. This lack of transparency introduces an element of uncertainty, making it difficult for users to track and reconcile their transactions.

Errors and mismatches, not uncommon in the complex web of correspondent banking, further compound the opacity issue. Discrepancies in transaction details, whether due to manual errors or system glitches, can lead to funds being held up or, in some cases, diverted to unintended destinations. The lack of a transparent and standardized tracking mechanism contributes to the prevalence of such errors, creating challenges for both senders and recipients.

Beneficiaries of cross-border payments, particularly in the case of remittances, suffer from the lack of clarity surrounding the arrival of funds. Dependence on the timely receipt of funds for essential needs, such as healthcare or education, magnifies the impact of these uncertainties. The current opacity in international transfers not only undermines the efficiency of the system but also erodes trust among participants.

As we navigate through these pain points ingrained in the current cross-border payment landscape, the urgency for a transformative solution becomes evident. The subsequent chapters will delve deeper into each of these challenges, exploring their intricacies and implications. In doing so, we will lay the foundation for understanding how Ripple envisions leveraging the XRP Ledger to address these issues and usher in a new era of efficiency, transparency, and accessibility in cross-border payments.

The need for improvement

In the ever-evolving landscape of global finance, the need for improvement in cross-border payments has become a resounding call to action. As we embark on a journey to explore the challenges and potential solutions, it is crucial to delve into the fundamental reasons driving the imperative for change. This chapter unravels the intricacies of the current cross-border payment systems, emphasizing the pressing need for improvement in speed, cost-effectiveness, accessibility, transparency, liquidity, interoperability, and overall efficiency.

The Imperative for Speed: A Time-Critical Global Economy

In a world where information travels at the speed of light, the sluggish pace of cross-border payments stands out as a glaring anomaly. The current systems, rooted in legacy technologies and encumbered by layers of intermediaries, struggle to keep pace with the demands of a fast-moving global economy.

The need for speed in cross-border payments extends beyond mere convenience. In today's interconnected world, businesses operate on a global scale, relying on timely and predictable fund transfers to meet operational needs. The delays inherent in the current systems result in missed opportunities, increased working capital requirements, and hinder the agility required to respond to dynamic market conditions.

Individuals, too, feel the impact of delayed transfers, especially in the context of remittances. Families dependent on timely remittance inflows for essential expenses such as education, healthcare, and daily living face disruptions when confronted with the current slow and unpredictable nature of cross-border transactions. The imperative for improvement in speed is not merely a desire for expediency; it is a necessity for fostering economic growth, financial inclusion, and overall global prosperity.

The Burden of Cost: A Barrier to Financial Inclusion

The cost associated with cross-border payments is a formidable barrier that obstructs the path to financial inclusion. High transaction fees, opaque foreign exchange spreads, and the overall lack of cost transparency contribute to an environment where the economic viability of cross-border transactions is compromised.

For businesses, especially small and medium-sized enterprises (SMEs), the burden of high transaction costs can be prohibitive. These businesses, often operating on tight budgets, find themselves at a disadvantage when engaging in international trade. The current cost structure not only limits the growth potential of these enterprises but also hinders their ability to compete on a level playing field with larger counterparts.

On an individual level, the high costs associated with cross-border transactions exacerbate financial disparities. The unbanked and underbanked, who can least afford excessive fees, find themselves excluded from participating in the global financial ecosystem. As we explore the need for improvement, it becomes evident that reducing the cost burden is not just an efficiency measure; it is a prerequisite for fostering a more inclusive and equitable financial landscape.

Access Denied: Bridging Gaps for the Unbanked and Emerging Markets

While digital advancements have brought the world closer, a significant portion of the global population remains excluded from the formal financial system. The unbanked and underbanked, residing predominantly in developing regions, face barriers that impede their ability to access cross-border payment services.

Improving access to cross-border payment systems is not merely about convenience; it is a catalyst for economic development. The unbanked, when granted access to affordable and efficient cross-border transactions, can engage more actively in international trade, remittances, and other financial activities. This, in turn, contributes to poverty alleviation and empowers communities with the tools to build a sustainable future.

Emerging markets, poised for growth and integration into the global economy, face significant friction when attempting to navigate the complexities of current cross-border payment systems. Simplifying access for businesses in these markets is paramount for unlocking their full economic potential. The need for improvement, therefore, extends beyond technical enhancements; it encompasses the removal of barriers that inhibit the full participation of individuals and businesses on a global scale.

The Quest for Transparency: Building Trust in Financial Transactions

Trust is the bedrock of any financial system, and transparency is its cornerstone. However, the current cross-border payment mechanisms often operate in the shadows, with limited visibility into transaction status and fee structures. This lack of transparency breeds uncertainty, erodes trust, and leaves participants in the payment chain vulnerable to errors and discrepancies.

Improving transparency in cross-border payments is not only about providing users with real-time information on the status of their transactions but also about demystifying fee structures. Users should have a clear understanding of the costs associated with their transactions, including foreign exchange spreads and intermediary fees. Transparent systems instill confidence, enabling users to make informed decisions and plan their financial activities effectively.

The opacity in international transfers also contributes to errors and mismatches, leading to funds being held up or misdirected. These errors not only inconvenience users but also result in additional costs and time-consuming reconciliation processes. As we explore the need for improvement, it becomes apparent that transparency is not just a desirable feature; it is a prerequisite for building a robust and trustworthy cross-border payment ecosystem.

The Crucial Role of Liquidity: Mitigating Volatility and Unleashing Capital

Volatility in currency markets poses a significant challenge to the stability of cross-border payments. The current reliance on pre-funded nostro accounts, where financial institutions hold reserves in foreign currencies, ties up significant amounts of capital that could otherwise be deployed for productive use. This practice not only incurs opportunity costs but also amplifies the impact of currency fluctuations on the overall cost of cross-border transactions.

Improving liquidity in cross-border payments is essential for mitigating the effects of currency volatility. A system that can provide on-demand liquidity, without the need for pre-funded accounts, enables financial institutions to optimize their capital usage. This, in turn, contributes to cost reduction, as the capital locked in nostro accounts can be channeled towards more productive endeavors.

Moreover, improved liquidity enhances the efficiency of cross-border payments by reducing the time and friction associated with capital movements. It enables transactions to occur in real-time, aligning with the expectations set by modern, digitally-driven economies. The need for improvement, therefore, extends to reshaping the liquidity landscape, fostering a system that is agile, responsive, and adaptive to the dynamic nature of global financial markets.

Navigating Interoperability Challenges: Fostering Seamless Transactions

In a world where interconnectedness is the norm, the current lack of interoperability in cross-border payment systems stands as a major impediment. Siloed payment networks, each with its own set of rules and protocols, hinder the seamless flow of transactions across borders. The absence of standardized communication and settlement mechanisms results in increased friction, delays, and inefficiencies.

Improving interoperability is not just about connecting disparate systems; it is about establishing a common language for cross-border transactions. Standardization of protocols and the development of interoperable frameworks enable different payment networks to communicate seamlessly. This, in turn, eliminates the need for complex partnerships and facilitates a more fluid and efficient cross-border payment ecosystem.

The current lack of interoperability particularly affects businesses and individuals engaging in cross-network transactions. The friction arising from incompatible systems not only leads to delays but also adds an additional layer of complexity, making it challenging for users to navigate the intricacies of the current cross-border payment landscape. As we explore the need for improvement, addressing interoperability challenges emerges as a fundamental step towards building a more connected and accessible global financial infrastructure.

The Unsustainability of the Status Quo: A Call for Modernization

The pain points ingrained in the current cross-border payment systems collectively paint a picture of an unsustainable status quo. The inefficiencies, delays, high costs, lack of transparency, limited access, and other challenges outlined in the preceding sections underscore the urgency for modernization. The landscape has evolved, and the demand for cross-border transactions to align with the speed, efficiency, and transparency of domestic transactions has never been more pronounced.

Incumbent systems, rooted in legacy technologies and processes, face increasing pressure to adapt to the changing dynamics of the global economy. The emergence of innovative technologies, coupled with a regulatory push for improvements, signals a paradigm shift in the cross-border payment space. The need for modernization is not just a response to market demands; it is a strategic imperative for financial institutions, regulators, and stakeholders to remain relevant in a rapidly evolving landscape.

As we transition from an exploration of the pain points to a discussion on potential solutions, it is essential to keep in mind the imperative for improvement. The ensuing chapters will delve into Ripple's vision for leveraging the XRP Ledger to address these challenges systematically. The goal is not merely to refine existing systems but to usher in a new era where cross-border payments are characterized by speed, efficiency, transparency, accessibility, and overall responsiveness to the needs of a globalized and interconnected world.

Chapter 1: Speed of International Transfers
Contrasting domestic and global transfer times

In the interconnected tapestry of global commerce, the speed of financial transactions is a crucial determinant of efficiency and competitiveness. As we delve into the nuances of international transfers, a glaring discrepancy comes to the forefront – the stark contrast between the swiftness of domestic transactions and the languid pace of their global counterparts. This chapter aims to dissect the factors contributing to this divergence, shedding light on the technological and systemic intricacies that hinder the speed of international transfers.

The Swift Pace of Domestic Transactions

Domestic transactions, facilitated within the confines of a single country, have undergone a remarkable transformation in recent years. The advent of real-time payment systems and advancements in technology has catapulted domestic transfers into a realm of immediacy and efficiency. In many developed economies, domestic transactions occur in real-time, allowing funds to move seamlessly between accounts within seconds.

The key to the rapid pace of domestic transactions lies in the streamlined nature of the systems governing them. In a domestic setting, financial institutions operate within a shared regulatory framework, and standardized communication protocols enable the swift movement of funds. Real-time gross settlement (RTGS) systems, where transactions are settled immediately and individually, have become commonplace, fostering an environment where the speed of transactions is limited only by the speed of technology.

Moreover, the absence of cross-border complexities further contributes to the speed of domestic transactions. In a closed-loop system, where all participants adhere to the same set of rules and regulations, the challenges inherent in navigating diverse legal, regulatory, and operational landscapes are non-existent. This lack of complexity allows domestic transactions to be executed seamlessly, setting a benchmark for speed and efficiency.

The Labyrinth of Global Transfer Times

Contrasting with the expeditious nature of domestic transactions, international transfers find themselves ensnared in a labyrinth of complexities that impede their speed. The challenges begin with the fundamental differences between domestic and international financial infrastructures.

In the realm of international transfers, the involvement of multiple jurisdictions, regulatory frameworks, and financial institutions introduces layers of complexity. Each intermediary bank in the correspondent banking model adds its own processing time, contributing to the overall delay. The need for compliance with diverse and often stringent regulatory requirements further elongates the processing time, as financial institutions navigate through a myriad of rules governing cross-border transactions.

Additionally, the reliance on legacy technologies in international payment systems exacerbates the speed challenge. Many of the existing systems were designed in an era when the concept of instantaneous global transactions seemed like a distant dream. The use of batch processing, where transactions are grouped together for processing at specific intervals, introduces delays that are inconceivable in the context of real-time expectations set by modern economies.

Currency conversion, an inherent aspect of international transactions, introduces an additional layer of complexity. The need to convert funds from one currency to another often involves multiple parties, each applying their own foreign exchange rates and fees. The lack of a standardized and transparent approach to currency conversion adds friction to the process, leading to delays and uncertainties.

The disparities in time zones further compound the challenges of international transfers. While the sun never sets on the global financial markets, the 24-hour nature of international business introduces complexities in terms of processing times. The need to coordinate and synchronize operations across different time zones adds an additional layer of intricacy, contributing to delays in the settlement of international transactions.

Technological Limitations and Outdated Infrastructure

The speed of international transfers is intricately tied to the technological capabilities and infrastructure underpinning the financial systems. In many cases, the outdated nature of existing technologies becomes a bottleneck, hindering the realization of faster cross-border transactions.

Legacy systems, characterized by outdated architectures and protocols, struggle to keep pace with the demands of a digitally-driven world. These systems were not designed to accommodate the real-time, data-intensive nature of modern international transactions. The result is a mismatch between the expectations of users and the capabilities of the infrastructure, leading to delays and inefficiencies.

Moreover, the lack of interoperability between different payment systems and networks contributes to the slow pace of international transfers. In a global landscape where various financial institutions operate on disparate platforms, the seamless flow of information and funds becomes a formidable challenge. The absence of standardized communication protocols and settlement mechanisms adds friction to the process, impeding the speed at which transactions can be executed.

The Impact on Individuals and Businesses

The disparity in speed between domestic and international transfers has tangible implications for both individuals and businesses engaged in cross-border transactions. For individuals, especially those relying on remittances for essential expenses, the delay in fund availability can lead to disruptions in daily life. Educational expenses, healthcare bills, and other time-sensitive needs are often contingent on the prompt receipt of remitted funds. The current lag in international transfer times jeopardizes the timely fulfillment of these critical needs.

Businesses operating on a global scale face a different set of challenges. The delayed settlement of international transactions introduces uncertainty into cash flow management, hindering the ability to respond swiftly to market dynamics. In a world where agility is synonymous with competitiveness, the sluggish pace of international transfers places businesses at a disadvantage.

The impact is particularly pronounced in industries where just-in-time inventory management and rapid response to customer demands are paramount. Delays in receiving payments or settling transactions can disrupt supply chains, lead to stockouts, and erode customer trust. In an era where global markets are interconnected and interdependent, the inefficiencies in cross-border payment systems reverberate through the entire economic ecosystem.

The Ripple Effect: Ripple's Approach to Enhancing Speed

As we confront the disparities in transfer times between domestic and international transactions, Ripple's approach stands out as a potential catalyst for change. Ripple leverages blockchain technology, specifically the XRP Ledger, to address the inefficiencies ingrained in the current cross-border payment landscape.

The XRP Ledger introduces the concept of a decentralized and open-source blockchain, where transactions are validated through a consensus mechanism. This departure from traditional centralized systems allows for a more streamlined and direct path for funds to move between parties. The elimination of intermediaries, each contributing to processing time, lays the groundwork for a more expeditious cross-border payment ecosystem.

Moreover, XRP, the native digital asset of the XRP Ledger, plays a pivotal role in enhancing the speed of cross-border transactions. XRP serves as a bridge currency, facilitating the seamless exchange of value between different fiat currencies. The speed and efficiency of XRP transactions arise from its consensus algorithm, which enables settlement in a matter of seconds.

By leveraging blockchain technology and the XRP Ledger, Ripple envisions a future where cross-border transactions can occur with the same speed and efficiency as their domestic counterparts. The elimination of batch processing, reduction of intermediaries, and the instantaneous settlement offered by XRP contribute to a paradigm shift in the way international transfers are conducted.

In the subsequent chapters, we will delve deeper into the various elements of Ripple's vision, exploring how each component addresses the challenges outlined in this chapter. As we navigate the landscape of cross-border payments, the quest for enhanced speed emerges as a fundamental principle guiding Ripple's transformative approach to revolutionize the current state of international transfers.

Batch processing causes delays

In the intricate dance of global finance, the speed at which funds move across borders is a critical determinant of efficiency and responsiveness. As we navigate the nuances of international transfers, one significant bottleneck comes to the forefront — the practice of batch processing. This chapter delves into the complexities and drawbacks of batch processing in the context of cross-border payments, unraveling how this approach contributes to delays and inefficiencies that undermine the seamless flow of funds across the global economic landscape.

Understanding Batch Processing in Cross-Border Payments

Batch processing is a conventional method employed in various financial systems where multiple transactions are grouped together and processed simultaneously at scheduled intervals. In the realm of cross-border payments, this method introduces a fundamental misalignment with the expectations set by modern economies, where real-time transactions have become the norm.

The rationale behind batch processing is rooted in historical limitations of technology and infrastructure. In the early days of financial systems, processing large volumes of transactions in real-time was a computationally intensive task. Batch processing emerged as a pragmatic solution, allowing financial institutions to manage the flow of transactions in a more controlled and systematic manner.

In the context of cross-border payments, batch processing involves accumulating a set of transactions over a specified period before initiating the processing cycle. These transactions, often diverse in nature and destination, are bundled together and dispatched for settlement. This approach introduces inherent delays, as transactions must wait for the completion of the batch before proceeding to the next stage of the settlement process.

The Lags Introduced by Batch Processing

The delays introduced by batch processing in cross-border payments are multifaceted and impact various stages of the transaction lifecycle.

1. Accumulation Phase Delays:

- Transactions must wait in a queue until a predefined batch size is reached before processing can commence. This waiting period introduces a delay even before the settlement process begins.

- The accumulation phase may span several hours or even days, depending on the policies and procedures of the financial institutions involved. This delay is exacerbated when dealing with low-volume corridors or during periods of low transaction activity.

2. Limited Processing Frequency:

- The periodic nature of batch processing sets predetermined intervals for transaction settlement. This limited processing frequency is incongruent with the expectations of users accustomed to the immediacy of modern digital transactions.

- Users initiating cross-border payments during the period between batch cycles must endure prolonged waiting times, as their transactions are held in abeyance until the next processing window.

3. Global Time Zone Challenges:

- The global nature of cross-border payments introduces an additional layer of complexity when batch processing is employed. Transactions initiated in different time zones may be subjected to extended processing times, leading to a lack of synchronicity in the settlement process.

- The misalignment of processing times with global business hours creates windows of inactivity, hindering the continuous flow of transactions and contributing to overall inefficiency.

4. Impact on Fund Availability:

- Batch processing delays have a tangible impact on the availability of funds for both senders and recipients. The time elapsed between initiation and settlement introduces uncertainty, affecting liquidity management and posing challenges for individuals and businesses reliant on timely access to funds.

5. Reduced Operational Efficiency:

- Financial institutions operating within a batch processing framework must allocate resources and infrastructure to manage the complexities associated with periodic settlement cycles. This leads to reduced operational efficiency, as the institution must contend with the intricacies of managing and processing large batches of transactions.

6. Challenges for Regulatory Compliance:

- Batch processing introduces challenges in meeting regulatory requirements, especially in the context of real-time transaction monitoring and reporting. The delayed settlement of transactions may conflict with evolving regulatory expectations for timely and transparent financial transactions.

The Ripple Effect: Ripple's Approach to Eliminate Batch Processing

Ripple's vision for transforming cross-border payments stands as a departure from the traditional batch processing model. Leveraging blockchain technology, specifically the XRP Ledger, Ripple introduces a paradigm shift by eliminating the need for batch processing altogether.

In traditional systems, the reliance on batch processing is often a consequence of the need to aggregate transactions for efficiency in settlement. However, the decentralized and consensus-driven nature of the XRP Ledger enables a more streamlined and immediate settlement process. Each transaction is treated individually, and consensus is achieved in near real-time, eliminating the need for bundling transactions into batches.

The elimination of batch processing introduces several key advantages within the Ripple ecosystem:

1. Real-Time Settlement:

- Ripple's approach facilitates real-time settlement of transactions, aligning with the expectations set by modern economies. As soon as a transaction is validated through the consensus process on the XRP Ledger, it is considered settled, eliminating the delays associated with batch processing.

2. Continuous Transaction Flow:

- The absence of batch processing in Ripple's system allows for a continuous flow of transactions. Users can initiate and settle transactions at any time, unencumbered by predetermined batch cycles. This continuous flow enhances the overall efficiency and responsiveness of cross-border payments.

3. Enhanced Liquidity Management:

- Real-time settlement enables more effective liquidity management for financial institutions. Rather than holding funds in anticipation of batch settlement, institutions can optimize their capital usage, deploying funds for more productive purposes.

4. Immediate Fund Availability:

- The elimination of batch processing ensures that funds are available to recipients almost immediately after the initiation of a transaction. This immediacy is particularly crucial for individuals and businesses reliant on timely access to funds for essential needs.

5. Improved Operational Efficiency:

- Ripple's approach reduces the operational burden associated with managing and processing large batches of transactions. Financial institutions can allocate resources more efficiently, focusing on value-added activities rather than navigating the complexities of batch settlement cycles.

6. Compliance with Regulatory Expectations:

- The real-time nature of transactions on the XRP Ledger aligns with evolving regulatory expectations for transparency and immediacy in financial transactions. Ripple's system facilitates compliance with regulatory requirements, as transactions are settled in near real-time, providing timely and accurate information.

As we dissect the intricacies of batch processing and its impact on the speed of international transfers, Ripple's approach emerges as a beacon of innovation. The subsequent chapters will delve further into the components of Ripple's vision, exploring how the elimination of batch processing is a pivotal step towards redefining the cross-border payment landscape. The quest for speed, efficiency, and immediacy in international transfers finds resonance in Ripple's commitment to revolutionize the status quo and usher in a new era of seamless, real-time cross-border transactions.

Slow correspondent banking model

In the intricate web of global transactions, the speed at which funds move across borders is a defining factor for the efficiency and competitiveness of the financial ecosystem. As we scrutinize the dynamics of international transfers, a significant impediment to speed emerges—the slow correspondent banking model. This chapter dissects the complexities and drawbacks of the correspondent banking model in the context of cross-border payments, unraveling how this traditional approach contributes to delays and inefficiencies that hinder the swift flow of funds across the interconnected global financial landscape.

Decoding the Correspondent Banking Model

The correspondent banking model has long been a cornerstone of international payments, providing a framework through which financial institutions facilitate cross-border transactions. In this model, banks establish correspondent relationships with each other to act as intermediaries in the transmission of funds between the sender's bank and the recipient's bank. While this system has been instrumental in enabling global transactions, it comes with inherent inefficiencies that impede the speed of international transfers.

Layers of Intermediaries and Complex Routing: The correspondent banking model introduces multiple layers of intermediaries into the cross-border payment process. As a result, a single international transaction may involve several intermediary banks between the sender's bank and the recipient's bank. Each intermediary bank adds its own processing time, leading to a cumulative delay in the overall settlement process. The complex routing of funds through this network of intermediaries creates a convoluted path that can contribute to the elongated timeline of transactions.

Sequential Processing and Dependency: Traditional correspondent banking operates on a sequential processing model. Each intermediary bank in the chain must process the transaction before passing it on to the next. This sequential nature of the process introduces dependencies, where the overall speed of the transaction is contingent on the efficiency of each intermediary bank in the chain. Delays or bottlenecks at any stage of the process can reverberate through the entire transaction lifecycle.

Lack of Standardization: The correspondent banking model lacks standardized protocols for communication and settlement. Each bank may have its own set of procedures, formats, and systems for handling international transactions. The absence of a universal standard leads to fragmentation and inefficiencies, as banks must navigate diverse and often incompatible systems when processing cross-border payments. This lack of standardization contributes to delays and increases the complexity of reconciling transactions.

Inherent Opacity and Limited Visibility: The correspondent banking model often operates with limited transparency and visibility into the status of transactions. Participants in the payment chain, including both the sender and the recipient, may have limited access to real-time information about the progress of their funds. This opacity introduces uncertainty and makes it challenging for users to track and reconcile their transactions. The lack of transparency also contributes to the prevalence of errors and mismatches, further impeding the speed of international transfers.

Regulatory Compliance Challenges: Correspondent banking involves navigating a complex landscape of international regulations and compliance requirements. Financial institutions must adhere to various anti-money laundering (AML) and know your customer (KYC) regulations, adding an additional layer of scrutiny to cross-border transactions. The need to ensure compliance with diverse regulatory frameworks introduces delays, as banks must perform thorough due diligence checks before processing transactions.

Impact on Individuals and Businesses: The sluggish nature of the correspondent banking model has tangible implications for both individuals and businesses engaged in cross-border transactions. Individuals relying on timely remittances for essential expenses may experience delays that disrupt their plans for education, healthcare, and daily living. Businesses operating on a global scale face challenges in managing working capital, responding to market dynamics, and maintaining the agility required for success in a rapidly evolving economic landscape.

Ripple's Vision: Disrupting the Correspondent Banking Model

Ripple's approach to cross-border payments challenges the traditional correspondent banking model, aiming to inject speed, efficiency, and transparency into international transactions. By leveraging blockchain technology and the XRP Ledger, Ripple introduces a transformative vision that addresses the inherent drawbacks of the correspondent banking model.

Direct Transactions and Immediate Settlement: Ripple's vision advocates for direct transactions between financial institutions, eliminating the need for multiple intermediaries in the correspondent banking model. This direct approach reduces the number of handoffs in the payment chain, streamlining the settlement process and minimizing delays. Immediate settlement on the XRP Ledger further accelerates the overall speed of cross-border transactions.

Reduced Dependency on Intermediaries: By facilitating direct transactions, Ripple reduces the dependency on multiple intermediaries. Each transaction involves a direct link between the sender's and recipient's financial institutions, minimizing the sequential processing and dependencies inherent in the correspondent banking model. This reduction in complexity contributes to a more agile and responsive cross-border payment ecosystem.

Standardization Through Interledger Protocol (ILP): Ripple introduces the Interledger Protocol (ILP) to standardize the communication and settlement processes in cross-border payments. ILP provides a common framework that enables interoperability between different ledgers and payment networks. The adoption of ILP fosters a more standardized approach, eliminating the fragmentation and lack of interoperability associated with traditional correspondent banking.

Enhanced Transparency and Visibility: The use of blockchain technology and the XRP Ledger introduces enhanced transparency into cross-border payments. Participants in the payment chain gain real-time visibility into the status of their transactions, reducing uncertainties and providing a clear view of the entire process. The transparency offered by Ripple's approach addresses the opacity challenges inherent in the correspondent banking model.

Streamlined Regulatory Compliance: Ripple's vision incorporates a commitment to regulatory compliance while streamlining the associated processes. The use of blockchain technology allows for the secure and transparent recording of transaction details, aiding in regulatory reporting requirements. Ripple's approach seeks to provide financial institutions with the tools needed to meet compliance obligations without compromising on speed and efficiency.

The RippleNet Advantage: Ripple's network, known as RippleNet, serves as the infrastructure that facilitates seamless cross-border payments. RippleNet connects financial institutions globally, allowing them to transact directly with each other. The use of RippleNet, combined with the speed and efficiency of the XRP Ledger, forms the backbone of Ripple's vision to disrupt the correspondent banking model and redefine the landscape of international transfers.

Impact on Individuals and Businesses: Ripple's approach to cross-border payments has the potential to transform the experience for both individuals and businesses. By reducing delays and increasing the speed of transactions, Ripple's vision addresses the pain points associated with the correspondent banking model. Individuals can benefit from faster remittances, ensuring timely access to funds for essential needs. Businesses, operating in an environment that demands agility, can streamline their financial operations and respond more effectively to market dynamics.

As we navigate through the intricacies of the correspondent banking model and Ripple's transformative vision, the subsequent chapters will delve deeper into the various elements of Ripple's approach. The quest for speed in international transfers is central to Ripple's mission, and the disruption of traditional correspondent banking is a pivotal step toward realizing a future where cross-border payments are characterized by efficiency, transparency, and immediate settlement.

Impact of slow transfers on individuals and businesses

In the intricate tapestry of global finance, the speed at which funds traverse international borders is a critical factor influencing economic efficiency and individual well-being. As we scrutinize the complexities of international transfers, the impact of slow transfers on individuals and businesses comes to the forefront. This chapter delves into the tangible repercussions of delayed cross-border transactions, shedding light on how the lethargic pace inherent in the current systems reverberates through the lives of individuals and the operations of businesses across the world.

The Personal Toll on Individuals:

1. Disruptions in Daily Life: The delay in international transfers has profound implications for individuals relying on remittances for their day-to-day needs. Whether it's supporting education, covering healthcare expenses, or meeting daily living costs, the timely receipt of remitted funds is crucial. Slow transfers disrupt the rhythm of daily life, creating uncertainties and challenges in managing essential expenses.

2. Educational Hurdles: For many families, remittances play a pivotal role in funding education. Delays in receiving funds can jeopardize educational opportunities, affecting the ability of individuals to pursue learning and skill development. The impact is not just financial; it extends to the potential hindrance of educational aspirations and personal growth.

3. Healthcare Vulnerabilities: Timely access to funds is particularly critical in healthcare scenarios. Individuals relying on international transfers for medical expenses may face

challenges in accessing timely treatment or medications. The delay in funds can lead to vulnerabilities in managing health emergencies, impacting the well-being and recovery of individuals.

4. Uncertainties in Daily Planning: Slow transfers introduce uncertainties into the daily planning of individuals and their families. From budgeting for recurring expenses to making informed decisions about major life events, the lack of predictability in fund availability hampers the ability of individuals to plan and manage their financial lives effectively.

The Operational Challenges for Businesses:

1. Working Capital Constraints: Businesses engaged in international trade often face working capital constraints due to delayed cross-border transactions. The lag between the initiation and settlement of transactions ties up capital that could otherwise be utilized for operational needs, expansion, or investment. Working within limited capital constraints hinders the ability of businesses to seize opportunities and respond promptly to market dynamics.

2. Disruptions in Supply Chains: The inefficiencies in cross-border payments can disrupt the seamless functioning of global supply chains. Businesses, especially those relying on just-in-time inventory management, may face challenges in procuring raw materials or goods due to delays in payment and settlement. This disruption cascades through the supply chain, leading to potential stockouts and impacting overall operational efficiency.

3. Erosion of Competitiveness: In a globalized marketplace, the ability to operate efficiently and respond swiftly to market demands is a key determinant of competitiveness. Businesses experiencing delays in cross-border transactions may find themselves at a disadvantage compared to counterparts with more agile and responsive financial operations. The erosion of competitiveness can have long-term implications for the sustainability and growth of businesses.

4. Impact on Cash Flow Management: Delayed international transfers complicate cash flow management for businesses. The unpredictability in the timing of fund availability makes it challenging for businesses to plan and execute their financial strategies effectively. Managing day-to-day operations, meeting financial obligations, and navigating fluctuations in demand become more arduous in an environment characterized by slow transfers.

Global Economic Implications:

1. Reduced Economic Productivity: The collective impact of delayed international transfers on individuals and businesses contributes to reduced economic productivity. The inefficiencies in cross-border payments introduce friction into the global economic system, hindering the fluid movement of capital and impeding the efficient allocation of resources. This reduction in productivity has broader implications for the overall economic health of nations and the world.

2. Inhibiting Financial Inclusion: Slow transfers exacerbate challenges in achieving financial inclusion,

particularly in regions where access to efficient cross-border payment systems is already limited. Individuals and businesses in these regions face heightened barriers to participating in the global economy, limiting their opportunities for growth and development.

3. Impaired Economic Resilience: The resilience of economies in the face of external shocks depends on the efficiency and adaptability of their financial systems. Slow transfers introduce vulnerabilities that can amplify the impact of economic disruptions. Businesses operating with constrained working capital and individuals facing delays in accessing essential funds may find it harder to weather economic downturns.

Ripple's Response: Addressing the Human Impact of Slow Transfers:

Ripple's Mission to Enhance Financial Access: Ripple's mission goes beyond mere technological innovation; it encompasses a commitment to enhancing financial access and inclusivity. By addressing the human impact of slow transfers, Ripple seeks to create a financial ecosystem where individuals and businesses can thrive, unburdened by the inefficiencies of traditional cross-border payment systems.

RippleNet's Role in Empowering Businesses: RippleNet, Ripple's global network of financial institutions, plays a pivotal role in empowering businesses to overcome the challenges posed by slow transfers. Through direct and instantaneous transactions, RippleNet facilitates the seamless movement of funds, allowing businesses to operate with greater agility and responsiveness.

Enhancing Liquidity and Working Capital Management: Ripple's approach to cross-border payments aims to enhance liquidity and working capital management for businesses. By reducing the time between transaction initiation and settlement, Ripple enables businesses to optimize their capital usage, improving their financial resilience and ability to navigate dynamic market conditions.

Promoting Financial Inclusion: Ripple's vision aligns with the goal of promoting financial inclusion on a global scale. By providing efficient and accessible cross-border payment solutions, Ripple seeks to empower individuals and businesses in underserved regions, unlocking their potential for economic participation and growth.

Realizing the Vision of Speedy, Predictable Transactions: At the heart of Ripple's response to slow transfers is the vision of transforming cross-border payments into a realm characterized by speed, predictability, and efficiency. By harnessing the capabilities of blockchain technology and the XRP Ledger, Ripple aims to eliminate the hurdles that hinder the seamless flow of funds, both for individuals with personal financial aspirations and for businesses with ambitions to thrive in the global marketplace.

Conclusion: Towards a Swifter and Inclusive Financial Future:

As we reflect on the impact of slow transfers on individuals and businesses, it becomes evident that the challenges extend beyond the technical intricacies of cross-border payments. Ripple's commitment to addressing the human impact of these challenges represents a transformative approach that seeks to redefine the global financial landscape.

The subsequent chapters will delve deeper into Ripple's vision, exploring how each facet of its approach contributes to mitigating the impact of slow transfers. From empowering businesses with efficient cross-border transactions to promoting financial inclusion and enhancing economic resilience, Ripple's mission transcends the realm of technology, aspiring to create a future where the speed of international transfers aligns with the needs and aspirations of individuals and businesses worldwide.

Chapter 2: Cost of Cross-Border Payments
Expensive fees to send globally

In the vast landscape of global finance, the cost of cross-border payments stands as a significant barrier to the seamless movement of funds across borders. As we unravel the intricacies of international transactions, one glaring issue comes to the forefront: the expensive fees associated with sending money globally. This chapter delves into the various dimensions of these fees, dissecting how they impact individuals, businesses, and the broader economic landscape, and exploring innovative solutions, particularly Ripple's approach, aimed at alleviating the financial burden imposed by costly cross-border payment systems.

Understanding the Fee Structure:

Cross-border payments entail a complex web of intermediaries, each extracting fees for their role in facilitating the movement of funds. These fees are not only diverse but can also be hidden or poorly communicated, contributing to the overall cost burden borne by both senders and recipients. The fee structure in traditional cross-border payment systems is characterized by several key elements:

1. Transaction Fees: Transaction fees are charges imposed by financial institutions for the processing and facilitation of cross-border transactions. These fees vary widely and may include charges at the sender's and recipient's banks, as well as fees imposed by intermediary banks in the correspondent banking model. The cumulative effect of

transaction fees can significantly inflate the overall cost of international transfers.

2. Currency Conversion Fees: Currency conversion fees come into play when funds need to be converted from one currency to another during the cross-border transaction process. Financial institutions typically apply a margin to the foreign exchange rate, leading to additional costs for the sender and recipient. The lack of transparency in currency conversion fees exacerbates the financial burden on individuals and businesses engaging in international transactions.

3. Intermediary Bank Fees: The correspondent banking model, often employed in cross-border payments, introduces multiple intermediary banks into the transaction chain. Each of these intermediaries imposes fees for their services, contributing to the overall cost of the transaction. These fees may include processing fees, handling charges, and other miscellaneous costs, further complicating the fee structure.

4. Access Fees: Access fees are charges imposed by financial institutions for providing access to cross-border payment networks or systems. In some cases, these fees may be levied on both the sender's and recipient's sides, further increasing the financial burden on both parties involved in the transaction.

5. Opaque Fee Communication: A pervasive challenge in traditional cross-border payment systems is the lack of transparent communication regarding fees. Senders and recipients may not have a clear understanding of the fees

associated with their transactions, leading to unexpected costs and contributing to a lack of trust in the system.

The Impact on Individuals:

1. Diminished Remittance Value: Individuals relying on remittances as a lifeline may find the value of their remitted funds significantly diminished by the cumulative impact of fees. High transaction fees and currency conversion charges eat into the amount that ultimately reaches the recipient, negatively impacting their ability to meet essential needs and achieve financial goals.

2. Financial Exclusion: For individuals in regions with limited access to affordable cross-border payment services, expensive fees exacerbate the challenges of financial exclusion. The high cost of international transfers may discourage individuals from engaging in cross-border transactions altogether, limiting their opportunities for economic participation and financial growth.

3. Burden on Migrant Workers: Migrant workers, a significant demographic in the global workforce, often face disproportionate challenges due to expensive cross-border payment fees. These workers, who send a substantial portion of their earnings to support families back home, bear the brunt of high fees, impacting their ability to fulfill familial responsibilities and contribute to the economic well-being of their home countries.

4. Inequality in Access: The financial burden imposed by costly cross-border payment fees contributes to inequality in access to financial services. Individuals in economically

disadvantaged regions may face higher fees, limiting their ability to engage in international transactions on equal footing with their counterparts in more affluent regions.

The Operational Challenges for Businesses:

1. Increased Transaction Costs: Businesses engaged in international trade grapple with increased transaction costs associated with cross-border payments. The cumulative effect of transaction fees, currency conversion charges, and intermediary bank fees adds a layer of complexity and cost to the financial operations of businesses, impacting their profit margins and competitiveness.

2. Erosion of Profitability: The high cost of cross-border payments can erode the profitability of businesses, particularly those operating on thin margins. Small and medium-sized enterprises (SMEs) may find it challenging to absorb the financial impact of expensive fees, limiting their ability to reinvest in growth initiatives or respond to market fluctuations.

3. Disincentive for Global Expansion: The financial burden imposed by cross-border payment fees may act as a disincentive for businesses considering global expansion. The fear of high transaction costs can influence decisions related to entering new markets, forming international partnerships, or diversifying supply chains, hindering the ability of businesses to seize opportunities in the global marketplace.

4. Complexity in Financial Planning: The unpredictable nature of cross-border payment fees introduces complexity into financial planning for businesses. The lack of transparency in fee structures makes it challenging for businesses to accurately

forecast and budget for international transactions, leading to uncertainties in cash flow management.

The Global Economic Consequences:

1. Impact on Foreign Aid and Development: High cross-border payment fees have implications for foreign aid and development initiatives. The substantial reduction in the value of remittances, often a crucial source of income for developing nations, can hinder economic development and poverty alleviation efforts. The inefficiencies in the system act as a counterforce to the positive impact that remittances can have on global economic stability.

2. Trade Inefficiencies: The high cost of cross-border payments contributes to inefficiencies in international trade. Businesses may be reluctant to engage in cross-border transactions due to the financial burden imposed by fees, leading to a suboptimal allocation of resources and hindering the potential for mutually beneficial global trade.

3. Economic Inequality: The financial burden imposed by expensive cross-border payment fees contributes to economic inequality on a global scale. Regions with limited access to affordable financial services may find their economic growth stifled, perpetuating disparities in income, opportunities, and access to resources.

Ripple's Response: Reducing the Financial Burden of Cross-Border Payments:

Ripple's Commitment to Lowering Costs: At the core of Ripple's mission is a commitment to reducing the financial burden associated with cross-border payments. Ripple acknowledges the detrimental impact of expensive fees on individuals, businesses, and the global economy, and seeks to address these challenges through innovative solutions.

Direct Transactions and Fee Reduction: Ripple's approach involves facilitating direct transactions between financial institutions, eliminating the need for multiple intermediaries and reducing the associated fees. By streamlining the transaction process, Ripple aims to make cross-border payments more cost-effective for both senders and recipients.

Currency Efficiency with XRP: Ripple's use of the XRP Ledger introduces the digital asset XRP as a bridge currency, enabling efficient and low-cost currency conversion. The speed and cost-effectiveness of XRP transactions contribute to reducing the overall cost of cross-border payments, making it a viable solution for financial institutions looking to optimize their operations.

Transparent Fee Communication: Ripple advocates for transparent fee communication in cross-border payments. By providing clear and accessible information about transaction fees, financial institutions using Ripple's technology empower their customers with a better understanding of the cost structure associated with international transfers. This transparency enhances trust and fosters more informed decision-making.

Conclusion: Paving the Way for Affordable Cross-Border Payments:

As we navigate the landscape of the cost of cross-border payments, it becomes evident that the financial burden associated with expensive fees extends far beyond transactional nuances. Ripple's vision of a more affordable and accessible cross-border payment ecosystem is not just a technological aspiration but a commitment to addressing the real-world challenges faced by individuals, businesses, and the global economy.

The subsequent chapters will delve deeper into how Ripple's approach, particularly through its innovative use of blockchain technology and the XRP Ledger, contributes to the reduction of costs in cross-border payments. From enhancing transparency in fee structures to introducing efficient currency conversion, Ripple's mission is intricately woven into the fabric of creating a future where the financial barriers to global transactions are dismantled, and the benefits of a connected global economy are accessible to all.

Foreign exchange spreads

In the intricate world of global finance, the cost of cross-border payments is a multifaceted challenge, with foreign exchange spreads emerging as a crucial component. As we dissect the intricacies of international transactions, the impact of foreign exchange spreads on the overall cost structure becomes apparent. This chapter explores the nuances of foreign exchange spreads, unraveling how these spreads contribute to the expenses incurred by individuals, businesses, and the global economy in the realm of cross-border payments. Additionally, it delves into Ripple's innovative approach, which aims to mitigate the impact of foreign exchange spreads and enhance the cost-effectiveness of cross-border transactions.

Understanding Foreign Exchange Spreads:

Foreign exchange spreads, often referred to as bid-ask spreads, represent the difference between the buying (bid) and selling (ask) prices of a currency pair. In the context of cross-border payments, where transactions involve the conversion of one currency into another, foreign exchange spreads play a pivotal role in determining the actual cost of the transaction. Key aspects of foreign exchange spreads include:

1. Bid and Ask Prices: The bid price represents the maximum price a buyer is willing to pay for a particular currency, while the ask price is the minimum price a seller is willing to accept. The difference between these two prices constitutes the foreign exchange spread. Financial institutions facilitate currency conversion for cross-border payments by offering these bid and ask prices to their customers.

2. Market Dynamics and Liquidity: Foreign exchange spreads are influenced by market dynamics and liquidity conditions. In highly liquid and actively traded currency pairs, spreads tend to be narrower, reflecting the ease with which currencies can be bought or sold. Conversely, in less liquid or volatile markets, spreads may widen as a risk management measure by financial institutions.

3. Brokerage and Dealer Markup: Financial institutions acting as intermediaries in cross-border payments often charge a markup on the interbank exchange rate to cover their operational costs and generate profit. This additional margin contributes to the widening of foreign exchange spreads. The level of markup can vary among institutions and may not always be transparent to the end-users.

4. Impact on Transaction Costs: The foreign exchange spread directly influences the transaction costs associated with currency conversion in cross-border payments. A wider spread results in higher costs for both the sender and the recipient, as the effective exchange rate deviates more from the interbank rate. The impact of foreign exchange spreads is particularly pronounced in transactions involving large amounts or frequent conversions.

The Impact on Individuals:

Foreign exchange spreads have tangible consequences for individuals engaging in cross-border transactions, influencing the affordability and accessibility of international financial interactions.

1. Diminished Remittance Value: Individuals relying on remittances from family members working abroad often experience the impact of foreign exchange spreads. The wider the spread, the lower the value of the remitted funds when converted into the local currency. This reduction in remittance value diminishes the financial support that individuals receive from their loved ones working in foreign countries.

2. Unpredictable Conversion Costs: The opacity surrounding foreign exchange spreads can make it challenging for individuals to predict the actual cost of converting currencies. Lack of transparency in fee structures and varying spreads across financial institutions contribute to uncertainty in conversion costs, impacting individuals' ability to budget and plan effectively.

3. Currency Volatility Concerns: Individuals may face additional challenges when dealing with currency volatility, as wider spreads often accompany periods of market instability. The fluctuation in exchange rates can lead to increased costs for individuals converting their funds, further emphasizing the need for transparency and cost-effective solutions in cross-border payments.

The Operational Challenges for Businesses:

Businesses engaged in international trade and cross-border transactions encounter specific challenges related to foreign exchange spreads, impacting their financial operations and competitiveness.

1. Erosion of Profit Margins: Foreign exchange spreads contribute to the overall transaction costs incurred by

businesses. The cumulative impact of wider spreads, in addition to other fees, can erode profit margins for businesses engaged in global commerce. Small and medium-sized enterprises (SMEs) operating on thin margins may find it particularly challenging to absorb these additional costs.

2. Unpredictable Currency Risks: The unpredictability of foreign exchange spreads introduces currency risks for businesses engaged in international transactions. Fluctuations in exchange rates, coupled with varying spreads, create challenges in accurately predicting the actual cost of cross-border payments. Businesses may need to implement risk management strategies to mitigate the impact of these uncertainties.

3. Competitive Disadvantages: Businesses operating in competitive global markets face challenges when dealing with wider foreign exchange spreads. Higher transaction costs can make their products or services less competitive compared to counterparts in regions where transaction costs are lower. This disadvantage may influence business decisions related to market expansion, pricing strategies, and overall competitiveness.

The Global Economic Implications:

The impact of foreign exchange spreads extends beyond individual transactions, contributing to broader economic consequences on a global scale.

1. Trade Imbalances: Wider foreign exchange spreads can contribute to trade imbalances between nations. Higher transaction costs and currency risks may deter some businesses

from engaging in cross-border trade, leading to a suboptimal allocation of resources and potential economic inefficiencies.

2. Market Distortions: The presence of wide foreign exchange spreads can distort market dynamics and hinder the efficient functioning of global financial markets. Market participants may face challenges in accessing fair and transparent exchange rates, impacting their ability to make informed financial decisions.

3. Inhibiting Economic Growth: The cumulative impact of costly cross-border payments, including wider foreign exchange spreads, can inhibit economic growth, particularly in regions heavily dependent on international trade. The financial barriers imposed by these costs may limit opportunities for economic development and global integration.

Ripple's Response: Mitigating the Impact of Foreign Exchange Spreads:

Ripple's approach to cross-border payments includes strategic measures to mitigate the impact of foreign exchange spreads, promoting transparency, efficiency, and cost-effectiveness.

1. Use of XRP as a Bridge Currency: Ripple leverages the digital asset XRP as a bridge currency to facilitate efficient and low-cost currency conversion. By providing a standardized and liquid intermediary, XRP minimizes the need for multiple currency conversions and reduces the impact of wider spreads on cross-border transactions. The speed and efficiency of XRP transactions contribute to overall cost savings.

2. Liquidity Solutions with On-Demand Liquidity (ODL): Ripple's On-Demand Liquidity (ODL) solution utilizes XRP to provide instant liquidity for cross-border payments. By sourcing liquidity in real-time through XRP transactions, financial institutions can reduce their reliance on pre-funded accounts in destination currencies. This strategic use of liquidity contributes to narrower spreads and more cost-effective currency conversions.

3. Real-Time Settlement: Ripple's commitment to real-time settlement on the XRP Ledger ensures that transactions are processed swiftly, minimizing exposure to exchange rate fluctuations. The immediacy of settlement contributes to more predictable and transparent costs for both senders and recipients, reducing the impact of foreign exchange spreads on the overall transaction.

4. Enhanced Transparency: Ripple's approach emphasizes transparency in fee structures and currency conversion costs. By providing clear and accessible information about transaction fees and the use of XRP for currency conversion, financial institutions using Ripple's technology empower their customers with a more accurate understanding of the costs associated with cross-border payments.

Conclusion: Paving the Way for Transparent and Cost-Effective Cross-Border Payments:

Foreign exchange spreads represent a significant dimension of the cost of cross-border payments, impacting individuals, businesses, and the global economy. Ripple's innovative approach, centered around the use of XRP as a bridge currency and real-time settlement through the XRP Ledger, aims to address the challenges posed by wider spreads, promoting transparency and cost-effectiveness in the realm of international transactions.

The subsequent chapters will delve deeper into how Ripple's strategic measures, particularly those focused on mitigating the impact of foreign exchange spreads, contribute to the realization of a future where cross-border payments are characterized by efficiency, predictability, and accessibility for individuals and businesses worldwide.

Lack of transparency around fees

In the intricate web of global financial transactions, the lack of transparency around fees emerges as a critical challenge within cross-border payment systems. As we navigate through the complexities of international fund transfers, this chapter focuses on the opacity surrounding fees and how it compounds the overall cost burden for individuals, businesses, and the global economy. Delving into the various dimensions of fee-related obscurity, we explore the impact on stakeholders, the challenges it poses, and Ripple's innovative approach to fostering transparency and accountability in cross-border payments.

Fee Ambiguity: A Barrier to Informed Decisions:

Opaque Fee Structures: In traditional cross-border payment systems, fee structures are often opaque and complex. Financial institutions may impose a myriad of fees, including transaction fees, currency conversion fees, and intermediary fees. The lack of transparency around these charges makes it challenging for users to grasp the full cost of their transactions.

Hidden Costs and Markups: Beyond explicit fees, hidden costs and markups can further obscure the true expense of cross-border payments. Financial institutions may apply additional margins to foreign exchange rates, charge undisclosed handling fees, or introduce hidden costs at various stages of the transaction process. These concealed elements contribute to the overall lack of transparency and hinder users' ability to make informed decisions.

Variability in Fee Structures: Fee structures can vary significantly between financial institutions, and even within the same institution, depending on the type of transaction and the currencies involved. This variability adds a layer of complexity, making it difficult for users to anticipate and understand the specific fees associated with their cross-border transactions.

Impact on Individuals:

Unanticipated Costs for Remittances: Individuals relying on remittances for their livelihoods often bear the brunt of fee ambiguity. The lack of transparency around fees means that senders and recipients may not have a clear understanding of the costs involved in cross-border transactions. This can lead to unanticipated expenses and reduced remittance values, impacting the financial well-being of recipients.

Vulnerability of the Unbanked: The unbanked and underbanked populations, already facing challenges in accessing financial services, are particularly vulnerable to the lack of fee transparency. Without clear information on fees, individuals in these demographics may be reluctant to engage in cross-border transactions, limiting their participation in the global economy and hindering financial inclusion efforts.

Trust Deficit in Financial Institutions: The lack of transparency erodes trust in financial institutions. When users are unable to clearly understand the fees associated with their transactions, it diminishes their confidence in the financial system. This trust deficit can have lasting implications for individuals' willingness to use cross-border payment services.

Operational Challenges for Businesses:

Impact on Business Planning: Businesses engaged in international trade require predictability in their financial operations. The lack of transparency around cross-border payment fees introduces uncertainty into budgeting and financial planning. Businesses may find it challenging to accurately forecast costs and allocate resources efficiently in the absence of clear fee information.

Hidden Costs in Supply Chains: The opacity of fees extends to businesses involved in global supply chains. Hidden costs in cross-border payments can disrupt the efficiency of supply chain operations, leading to unanticipated expenses and challenges in managing working capital. This lack of transparency hampers the resilience and adaptability of businesses in the face of dynamic market conditions.

Complexity in Cost Analysis: Transparent fee structures are essential for businesses to conduct comprehensive cost analyses. The lack of clarity around fees complicates the evaluation of the true cost of cross-border transactions. Businesses may struggle to assess the competitiveness of different financial institutions and choose partners that align with their strategic objectives.

Global Economic Consequences:

Reduced Efficiency in Global Trade: Fee ambiguity contributes to reduced efficiency in global trade. Businesses may hesitate to engage in cross-border transactions due to concerns about undisclosed costs and unpredictable fee structures. This hesitancy limits the fluidity of international trade, hindering the efficient allocation of resources and impeding economic growth.

Inhibiting Financial Inclusion Goals: Fee opacity acts as a barrier to achieving financial inclusion goals globally. In regions where access to affordable financial services is already limited, the lack of fee transparency exacerbates challenges. Individuals and businesses in these regions may remain on the sidelines of the global economy, impeding efforts to reduce economic disparities.

Risk of Market Distortions: The lack of transparency in cross-border payment fees can contribute to market distortions. Financial institutions with non-transparent fee structures may gain a competitive advantage, leading to an uneven playing field. This dynamic can distort market dynamics and hinder fair competition, affecting the stability and integrity of the global financial system.

Ripple's Response: A Commitment to Transparency:

Clear Communication of Fees: Ripple's approach to cross-border payments places a strong emphasis on transparent fee structures. Financial institutions utilizing Ripple's technology are encouraged to provide clear and accessible information about the fees associated with cross-border transactions. This commitment to transparency enhances user understanding and fosters trust in the financial system.

Real-Time Fee Information: Ripple's technology facilitates the real-time communication of fee information. By enabling financial institutions to relay fee details to users instantly, Ripple ensures that individuals and businesses have up-to-date information on the costs of their transactions. Real-time fee information enhances the overall user experience and supports informed decision-making.

Standardized Fee Models: Ripple promotes the use of standardized fee models to simplify the fee structure for cross-border payments. Standardization enhances clarity for users, making it easier to compare costs between different financial institutions. This approach contributes to a more competitive and user-friendly cross-border payment ecosystem.

Conclusion: Illuminating the Path to Transparent Cross-Border Payments:

The lack of transparency around fees in cross-border payments is a pervasive challenge that affects individuals, businesses, and the global economy. Ripple's commitment to transparency represents a pivotal step toward illuminating this complex landscape. By championing clear communication, real-time fee information, and standardized fee models, Ripple seeks to empower users, foster trust, and contribute to a cross-border payment ecosystem characterized by openness, fairness, and accessibility.

As we journey through the subsequent chapters, we will delve deeper into how Ripple's dedication to transparency aligns with its broader mission to revolutionize cross-border payments. From addressing the impact on individuals and businesses to contributing to the efficiency of global trade, Ripple's approach represents a transformative force in the ongoing evolution of the international financial landscape.

High costs deter use cases

In the intricate world of cross-border payments, the specter of high costs looms large, casting a shadow over the potential use cases and applications of this vital financial infrastructure. This chapter delves into the multifaceted ways in which exorbitant costs associated with international transactions act as a deterrent, hindering the realization of various use cases. From remittances to global trade, the impact of high costs resonates across sectors, affecting individuals, businesses, and the broader global economy. As we navigate through the complexities of cost considerations, we explore Ripple's innovative approach aimed at dismantling these barriers and unlocking the full spectrum of cross-border payment use cases.

The Deterrent Effect of High Costs:

Understanding the Financial Implications: High costs in cross-border payments encompass a range of fees, including transaction fees, currency conversion fees, and intermediary fees. These costs can accumulate at each stage of the transaction process, from the initiation of the payment to its final settlement. The financial implications of these high costs are profound, impacting both senders and recipients and acting as a deterrent to the seamless flow of funds across borders.

Impact on Remittances: Remittances, a lifeline for many individuals and families, bear a significant burden due to high cross-border payment costs. The cumulative effect of transaction fees, currency conversion charges, and other associated costs diminishes the value of remitted funds. For individuals relying on remittances, these high costs translate into reduced financial support, hindering their ability to meet essential needs and achieve financial goals.

Challenges for Small and Medium-Sized Enterprises (SMEs): Small and medium-sized enterprises (SMEs) engaged in international trade face formidable challenges when confronted with high cross-border payment costs. The financial burden imposed by these costs impacts profit margins, operational efficiency, and the overall competitiveness of SMEs. For businesses operating on relatively thin margins, the deterrent effect of high costs can be particularly pronounced.

Inhibiting Global Trade: The world is interconnected through a complex web of global trade, and high cross-border payment costs present a substantial impediment. Businesses engaged in cross-border trade may face disincentives to expand their reach and explore new markets due to the fear of incurring exorbitant transaction fees. This inhibition limits the growth potential of global trade and introduces inefficiencies in the allocation of resources.

High Costs as a Barrier to Financial Inclusion:

Challenges for the Unbanked and Underbanked: The unbanked and underbanked populations, already facing challenges in accessing financial services, encounter heightened barriers due to high cross-border payment costs. For individuals in these demographics, the prospect of incurring significant fees acts as a deterrent to engaging in international financial transactions. This barrier exacerbates financial exclusion and impedes efforts to bring these populations into the formal financial ecosystem.

Reducing Access for Emerging Markets: Emerging markets, often characterized by vibrant economic activities, face the challenge of reduced access to global financial services due to high cross-border payment costs. The financial barriers imposed by these costs can deter businesses in emerging markets from participating in international trade and limit their ability to leverage global opportunities for growth.

Impact on Cross-Border E-Commerce: The rise of cross-border e-commerce, fueled by the digital era, encounters impediments in the form of high transaction costs. Online businesses operating in a global marketplace may find it economically unviable to cater to diverse international customer bases when faced with exorbitant cross-border payment fees. This limitation hampers the potential of cross-border e-commerce to become a truly inclusive and accessible phenomenon.

Ripple's Response: Lowering Costs to Unlock Use Cases:

The RippleNet Advantage: Ripple's approach to cross-border payments centers around the idea of lowering costs to unlock a multitude of use cases. Through its RippleNet network, financial institutions gain access to a streamlined and cost-effective infrastructure that minimizes the financial burden associated with international transactions. RippleNet facilitates direct transactions between financial institutions, eliminating the need for multiple intermediaries and reducing costs at each step.

On-Demand Liquidity (ODL): Ripple's On-Demand Liquidity (ODL) solution harnesses the power of the digital asset XRP to provide instant liquidity for cross-border payments. By sourcing liquidity in real-time through XRP transactions, financial institutions can minimize the need for pre-funded accounts in destination currencies. This strategic use of liquidity contributes to lower costs and enhances the efficiency of cross-border transactions.

Efficient Currency Conversion with XRP: Ripple's use of the XRP Ledger introduces the digital asset XRP as a bridge currency, facilitating efficient and low-cost currency conversion. XRP's speed and cost-effectiveness make it an ideal intermediary for cross-border payments, reducing the impact of high conversion costs associated with traditional currency exchange mechanisms.

Transparent Fee Structures: Ripple advocates for transparent fee structures within its network. Financial institutions utilizing Ripple's technology are encouraged to provide clear and accessible information about the fees associated with cross-border transactions. This commitment to transparency empowers users with a better understanding of the costs involved, fostering trust and informed decision-making.

Unlocking Cross-Border Payment Use Cases:

Enhancing Remittance Affordability: Ripple's focus on lowering costs has a direct impact on the affordability of remittances. By minimizing transaction fees and currency conversion costs, Ripple's technology ensures that the value of remitted funds remains closer to the sender's intended amount. This enhancement in affordability contributes to the well-being of individuals and families reliant on remittances.

Empowering SMEs in Global Trade: Small and medium-sized enterprises (SMEs) stand to gain significantly from the lower costs facilitated by Ripple's technology. The reduced financial burden associated with cross-border payments enhances the competitiveness of SMEs in global trade. Businesses can explore new markets, expand their reach, and participate more actively in international commerce.

Facilitating Financial Inclusion: Ripple's commitment to lowering costs aligns with the goal of fostering financial inclusion. By reducing the barriers imposed by high transaction costs, Ripple's technology opens up opportunities for the unbanked and underbanked to engage in cross-border transactions. This inclusivity aligns with global efforts to bring more individuals into the formal financial ecosystem.

Stimulating Cross-Border E-Commerce: The lower costs facilitated by Ripple's technology have the potential to stimulate cross-border e-commerce. Online businesses can operate more efficiently and profitably in a global marketplace where transaction costs are minimized. This stimulation of cross-border e-commerce contributes to economic growth and the democratization of international trade.

Conclusion: Lowering Costs, Expanding Possibilities:

High costs in cross-border payments act as a formidable deterrent, limiting the realization of diverse use cases across sectors. Ripple's innovative approach, focused on lowering costs through streamlined processes, digital assets like XRP, and transparent fee structures, seeks to dismantle these barriers. By enhancing affordability, empowering businesses, fostering financial inclusion, and stimulating e-commerce, Ripple's technology paves the way for a future where the full spectrum of cross-border payment use cases can be explored and realized. As we progress through subsequent chapters, we will further unravel how Ripple's commitment to cost-effectiveness aligns with its broader vision for transforming the landscape of international transactions.

Chapter 3: Access to Cross-Border Systems
Billions remain unbanked globally

In the evolving landscape of cross-border payments, one of the glaring challenges is the widespread lack of access to financial services, leaving billions unbanked globally. This chapter delves into the complexities of financial exclusion and how it acts as a significant barrier to participation in cross-border systems. From the root causes of global unbanked populations to the socio-economic implications, we explore the multifaceted nature of this challenge. Additionally, we examine how Ripple's innovative solutions are poised to address these issues, paving the way for greater financial inclusion and accessibility to cross-border systems.

The Global Unbanked Phenomenon:

Defining Financial Inclusion: Financial inclusion is a fundamental concept that encompasses providing access to affordable and appropriate financial services to all individuals, irrespective of their economic status. In the context of cross-border payments, financial inclusion extends beyond domestic boundaries, aiming to ensure that people globally can participate in the international financial system.

Billions Remain Unbanked: Despite advancements in technology and finance, a significant portion of the global population remains unbanked. According to various reports, billions of people lack access to basic financial services such as bank accounts, payment systems, and credit. The unbanked phenomenon is not confined to specific regions but is a global challenge with far-reaching consequences.

Root Causes of Financial Exclusion: The causes of financial exclusion are multifaceted and often rooted in socio-economic factors. Limited infrastructure, geographic remoteness, low income levels, lack of documentation, and cultural barriers contribute to the exclusion of individuals from formal financial systems. The unbanked face challenges in accessing banking services, saving for the future, and participating in economic activities beyond their immediate communities.

The Socio-Economic Impact:

Limited Economic Opportunities: The unbanked face limited economic opportunities due to their exclusion from formal financial systems. Without access to banking services, individuals may struggle to save, invest, or access credit. This limitation hampers their ability to start or expand businesses, hindering economic growth at both individual and community levels.

Financial Vulnerability: The unbanked are often more vulnerable to financial shocks and emergencies. The absence of formal banking channels makes it challenging for them to build financial resilience or access insurance products. As a result, unforeseen events, such as medical emergencies or natural disasters, can have disproportionate and long-lasting financial consequences.

Exclusion from Global Transactions: Financial exclusion extends beyond local economies, impacting individuals' ability to engage in global transactions. The unbanked are often sidelined from the benefits of cross-border trade, remittances, and international financial opportunities. This exclusion exacerbates global economic disparities and limits the potential for inclusive economic growth.

The Role of Cross-Border Payments in Financial Inclusion:

Importance of Cross-Border Financial Inclusion: Achieving financial inclusion on a global scale requires addressing barriers not only within domestic financial systems but also in cross-border transactions. Cross-border financial inclusion ensures that individuals in underserved regions can participate in the broader global economy, benefiting from international trade, remittances, and economic opportunities.

Challenges in Cross-Border Financial Inclusion: Cross-border financial inclusion presents unique challenges. The traditional correspondent banking model, characterized by multiple intermediaries and complex processes, can be a significant barrier for individuals in remote or underserved regions. Limited access to banking infrastructure, such as ATMs and branches, further complicates efforts to include individuals in cross-border financial systems.

Ripple's Vision for Inclusive Cross-Border Systems:

Overcoming Geographic Barriers: Ripple envisions a future where geographic barriers are overcome, and individuals in remote or underserved regions can seamlessly participate in cross-border transactions. Through its decentralized and digital solutions, Ripple aims to create an inclusive financial ecosystem that connects people globally, regardless of their location.

Streamlining Cross-Border Payments: The traditional correspondent banking model is known for its inefficiencies and complexities, often resulting in high costs and slow transaction times. Ripple's approach involves streamlining cross-border payments by facilitating direct transactions between financial institutions. This reduces the need for multiple intermediaries, leading to faster and more cost-effective international transfers.

Digital Assets for Financial Inclusion: Ripple's use of digital assets, such as XRP, plays a crucial role in enhancing financial inclusion. Digital assets provide a bridge between different currencies, enabling efficient and low-cost currency conversion. This is particularly beneficial for individuals in regions where access to traditional banking infrastructure is limited. By leveraging digital assets, Ripple contributes to the vision of a more inclusive cross-border payment system.

Empowering the Unbanked:

Ripple's On-Demand Liquidity (ODL) Solution: Ripple's On-Demand Liquidity (ODL) solution, which utilizes the digital asset XRP, offers a transformative approach to cross-border payments. ODL enables financial institutions to source liquidity in real-time through XRP transactions, eliminating the need for pre-funded accounts in destination currencies. This strategic use of liquidity enhances the efficiency of cross-border transactions, making them more accessible to the unbanked.

Facilitating Remittances: Remittances, a vital source of financial support for many families, can be more accessible and affordable through Ripple's solutions. By reducing the costs and complexities associated with cross-border payments, Ripple's technology empowers individuals to send and receive remittances with greater ease. This not only benefits the recipients but also stimulates economic activities in regions dependent on remittance inflows.

Unlocking Economic Opportunities: Ripple's vision includes unlocking economic opportunities for the unbanked by providing them with the tools to participate in the global economy. Through streamlined cross-border payments, digital assets, and decentralized financial infrastructure, Ripple aims to break down barriers and empower individuals to engage in economic activities beyond their immediate communities.

Conclusion: Towards a Globally Inclusive Financial Ecosystem:

The global challenge of financial exclusion, particularly the unbanked phenomenon, is a significant hurdle in the path towards a truly inclusive cross-border financial ecosystem. Ripple's innovative solutions, driven by the vision of a more connected and accessible world, are strategically designed to address these challenges. By streamlining cross-border payments, leveraging digital assets, and empowering the unbanked, Ripple is contributing to the realization of a future where individuals, regardless of their geographic location or economic status, can participate in the global financial landscape. As we progress through subsequent chapters, we will further explore how Ripple's commitment to inclusive cross-border systems aligns with its broader mission of transforming the way we think about and engage in international transactions.

Friction for emerging markets

In the intricate realm of cross-border payments, the challenges faced by emerging markets create friction that hinders their seamless integration into global financial systems. This chapter explores the specific hurdles and complexities that emerging markets encounter in their quest for access to cross-border systems. From infrastructural limitations to regulatory uncertainties, we delve into the nuanced landscape of emerging markets. Additionally, we examine how Ripple's innovative solutions are poised to alleviate these frictions, unlocking opportunities for financial inclusion and participation in the broader international economy.

The Dynamics of Emerging Markets:

Defining Emerging Markets: Emerging markets, often referred to as developing economies, represent countries that are in the process of rapid industrialization and experiencing significant economic growth. These markets are characterized by a transition from traditional to more modern economic structures and often face unique challenges as they seek to integrate into the global financial ecosystem.

The Promise and Challenges: Emerging markets hold great promise for economic growth and global contributions. However, they also grapple with a myriad of challenges that impede their smooth participation in cross-border systems. These challenges range from infrastructural limitations to regulatory complexities, creating friction that requires strategic solutions for sustainable development.

Friction Points for Emerging Markets:

Limited Financial Infrastructure: One of the primary sources of friction for emerging markets is the limited financial infrastructure. In many cases, these markets lack robust banking systems, ATMs, and digital payment infrastructure that are essential components of efficient cross-border transactions. The absence of such infrastructure complicates the process of sending and receiving international payments, hindering economic activities on a global scale.

Currency Volatility and Risk: Emerging markets often grapple with currency volatility, introducing an element of risk into cross-border transactions. Fluctuating exchange rates can result in unpredictable costs for businesses and individuals engaged in international trade or remittances. The inherent risk associated with currency volatility can act as a deterrent, discouraging participation in cross-border financial activities.

Regulatory Uncertainties: Regulatory environments in emerging markets are often characterized by uncertainties and complexities. The lack of clear and consistent regulations governing cross-border payments can create challenges for financial institutions, businesses, and individuals seeking to engage in international transactions. Regulatory uncertainties introduce friction by adding layers of complexity to compliance and legal processes.

Limited Access to Banking Services: A significant portion of the population in emerging markets may have limited access to formal banking services. This exclusion from traditional financial institutions makes it challenging for individuals to participate in cross-border transactions. Limited access to banking services impedes financial inclusion efforts and hampers the ability of individuals to leverage international economic opportunities.

Socio-Economic Impact on Emerging Markets:

Reduced Economic Opportunities: Friction in cross-border systems directly translates to reduced economic opportunities for emerging markets. Businesses face challenges in expanding their operations globally, limiting their potential for growth and market diversification. The inability to seamlessly engage in cross-border transactions may result in missed opportunities for economic development and diversification.

Impact on Remittances: Remittances play a crucial role in the economies of many emerging markets, serving as a significant source of financial support for families. Friction in cross-border systems can impact the affordability and accessibility of remittances, reducing the overall financial well-being of individuals and communities dependent on these funds.

Disincentive for Foreign Direct Investment (FDI): Friction in cross-border systems acts as a disincentive for foreign direct investment (FDI) in emerging markets. Businesses and investors may be hesitant to engage in cross-border transactions with entities in these markets due to uncertainties, risks, and complexities. This reluctance hampers the flow of capital and inhibits economic development.

Ripple's Approach to Alleviating Friction:

Enhancing Financial Infrastructure: Ripple's innovative solutions are designed to enhance financial infrastructure, particularly in regions facing limitations. By providing a decentralized and digital framework for cross-border payments, Ripple contributes to the development of a more efficient and inclusive financial infrastructure. The use of technologies like the XRP Ledger and On-Demand Liquidity (ODL) streamlines transactions, reducing the reliance on traditional banking infrastructure.

Mitigating Currency Volatility: Ripple's approach to mitigating friction in emerging markets includes addressing currency volatility. The use of the digital asset XRP as a bridge currency facilitates swift and cost-effective currency conversion. By providing a stable and standardized intermediary, Ripple's technology helps reduce the impact of currency volatility, making cross-border transactions more predictable and accessible.

Navigating Regulatory Challenges: Ripple actively engages with regulatory bodies globally to navigate the regulatory challenges faced by emerging markets. By advocating for clear and consistent regulations, Ripple aims to create an environment that fosters innovation and encourages the adoption of digital solutions in cross-border payments. Clarity in regulations reduces uncertainties, promoting a more favorable environment for financial institutions and businesses.

Expanding Access to Banking Services: Ripple's commitment to financial inclusion extends to expanding access to banking services in emerging markets. Through its solutions,

Ripple aims to empower individuals in these markets with greater access to formal financial services. By connecting financial institutions globally, Ripple facilitates improved access to banking services, creating opportunities for economic participation.

Empowering Emerging Markets:

Stimulating Economic Growth: Ripple's vision includes stimulating economic growth in emerging markets by reducing friction in cross-border transactions. Streamlining the international payment process enables businesses in these markets to engage more actively in global trade, attracting foreign investments and fostering economic development. The ripple effect extends beyond individual transactions to contribute to the overall growth of emerging market economies.

Enhancing Remittance Affordability: Ripple's focus on alleviating friction directly benefits the affordability of remittances for individuals in emerging markets. By reducing transaction costs and providing more efficient currency conversion, Ripple's technology ensures that remittance recipients receive a larger portion of the funds sent by their relatives abroad. This enhancement in affordability contributes to improved financial well-being for recipients in emerging markets.

Attracting Foreign Investments: Reducing friction in cross-border systems through Ripple's solutions creates a more attractive environment for foreign investments in emerging markets. Businesses and investors are more likely to participate in cross-border transactions when faced with fewer obstacles and uncertainties. This increased confidence in the reliability and efficiency of the financial infrastructure contributes to the attraction of foreign capital.

Conclusion: Navigating Friction for a Connected Future:

Friction in cross-border systems poses unique challenges for emerging markets, hindering their seamless integration into the global financial ecosystem. Ripple's innovative solutions, driven by a commitment to enhancing financial infrastructure, mitigating currency volatility, navigating regulatory challenges, and expanding access to banking services, are strategically positioned to alleviate these frictions. By empowering emerging markets, Ripple contributes to a future where these regions can actively participate in and benefit from the opportunities presented by cross-border transactions. As we progress through subsequent chapters, we will further explore how Ripple's approach aligns with its broader mission of transforming the landscape of international transactions and fostering global financial inclusion.

Small businesses struggle with access

In the intricate web of cross-border payments, small businesses emerge as significant players facing unique challenges in accessing international financial systems. This chapter delves into the nuanced landscape of small businesses struggling with access to cross-border systems. From limited resources to complex processes, we explore the specific hurdles that impede the seamless participation of small enterprises in global transactions. Additionally, we examine how Ripple's innovative solutions are strategically positioned to address these challenges, offering a pathway for small businesses to overcome obstacles and engage more actively in the international economic landscape.

The Vital Role of Small Businesses:

Driving Economic Activity: Small businesses play a pivotal role in driving economic activity globally. They contribute to job creation, innovation, and economic growth, forming the backbone of many economies. In an increasingly interconnected world, the ability of small businesses to engage in cross-border transactions is crucial for their expansion, sustainability, and competitiveness.

Challenges Faced by Small Businesses: While small businesses are key contributors to economic vitality, they often face unique challenges in the realm of cross-border payments. Limited financial resources, operational complexities, and barriers to entry into global markets create hurdles that can be daunting for small enterprises seeking to navigate the intricacies of international transactions.

Challenges for Small Businesses Accessing Cross-Border Systems:

Limited Financial Resources: Small businesses typically operate with limited financial resources, making the cost of engaging in cross-border transactions a significant concern. High transaction fees, currency conversion costs, and the need for pre-funded accounts can strain the already constrained budgets of small enterprises. These financial barriers hinder their ability to compete globally and explore new markets.

Complexity of International Payments: The complexity of international payment processes poses a significant challenge for small businesses. Traditional correspondent banking models often involve multiple intermediaries, intricate documentation, and extended settlement times. Navigating these complexities can be overwhelming for small enterprises with limited administrative capacity and financial expertise.

Currency Exchange Risks: Small businesses are particularly vulnerable to currency exchange risks. Fluctuating exchange rates can result in unpredictable costs, impacting the profitability of cross-border transactions. The absence of risk mitigation strategies and the ability to navigate the complexities of currency exchange introduce uncertainties that small businesses may find challenging to address.

Limited Access to Banking Services: Access to banking services is a critical factor for small businesses engaging in cross-border transactions. In regions where formal banking infrastructure is limited, small enterprises may face challenges in establishing relationships with financial institutions that facilitate international payments. Limited access to banking services restricts the options available to small businesses for cross-border transactions.

Socio-Economic Impact on Small Businesses:

Reduced Global Competitiveness: Friction in accessing cross-border systems directly translates to reduced global competitiveness for small businesses. Competing on an international scale requires efficient and cost-effective means of engaging in cross-border transactions. The challenges faced by small enterprises in this regard can hinder their ability to compete with larger counterparts and capitalize on global market opportunities.

Missed Growth Opportunities: The ability to access cross-border systems is closely tied to small businesses' capacity for expansion and growth. When faced with obstacles in international transactions, small enterprises may miss opportunities to enter new markets, form strategic partnerships, and diversify their customer base. These missed growth opportunities have lasting implications for the long-term sustainability of small businesses.

Operational Inefficiencies: The complexities and barriers in accessing cross-border systems introduce operational inefficiencies for small businesses. Lengthy transaction times, manual processes, and uncertainties related to costs can disrupt day-to-day operations. Small enterprises may find themselves allocating significant resources to navigate these challenges, diverting attention from core business activities.

Ripple's Approach to Empowering Small Businesses:

Reducing Transaction Costs: One of the primary focuses of Ripple's innovative solutions is the reduction of transaction costs, a critical concern for small businesses. By streamlining cross-border payments and minimizing the need for multiple intermediaries, Ripple's technology aims to make international transactions more cost-effective. This reduction in transaction costs directly benefits small enterprises, enabling them to allocate resources more efficiently.

Efficient Currency Conversion: Ripple's approach to efficient currency conversion addresses a significant challenge faced by small businesses engaged in cross-border transactions. Through the use of the digital asset XRP as a bridge currency, Ripple facilitates swift and cost-effective currency conversion. This strategic use of digital assets contributes to minimizing currency exchange risks and reducing the complexities associated with fluctuating exchange rates.

Streamlining International Payment Processes: Ripple's technology is designed to streamline international payment processes, making them more accessible and user-friendly for small businesses. By providing a decentralized and digital framework, Ripple minimizes the complexities associated with traditional correspondent banking models. Small enterprises can benefit from faster settlement times, reduced administrative burdens, and a more straightforward approach to engaging in cross-border transactions.

Enhancing Access to Banking Services: Ripple's commitment to enhancing access to banking services aligns with the needs of small businesses. Through its solutions, Ripple aims to connect financial institutions globally, creating a network that facilitates improved access to formal banking services. This connectivity expands the options available to small enterprises for engaging in cross-border transactions, fostering financial inclusion on a global scale.

Empowering Small Businesses in Cross-Border Transactions:

Stimulating Global Competitiveness: Ripple's technology stimulates global competitiveness for small businesses by addressing key challenges in cross-border transactions. Reduced transaction costs, efficient currency conversion, and streamlined payment processes contribute to enhancing the competitiveness of small enterprises. This empowerment enables them to participate more actively in global markets, compete with larger counterparts, and explore new opportunities.

Facilitating Market Expansion: Small businesses are empowered to explore new markets and expand their reach through Ripple's solutions. By providing a more accessible and efficient framework for cross-border transactions, Ripple facilitates market expansion for small enterprises. This not only contributes to their growth but also stimulates economic activities in regions that may have been previously underserved.

Mitigating Currency Exchange Risks: Ripple's approach to mitigating currency exchange risks directly benefits small businesses engaged in international transactions. The use of

XRP as a bridge currency introduces stability and efficiency into the currency conversion process, minimizing the impact of fluctuating exchange rates. Small enterprises can navigate cross-border transactions with greater predictability, reducing the uncertainties associated with currency risks.

Conclusion: A Pathway for Small Businesses in a Connected World:

The challenges faced by small businesses in accessing cross-border systems are complex and multifaceted. Ripple's innovative solutions, driven by a commitment to reducing transaction costs, efficient currency conversion, streamlining payment processes, and enhancing access to banking services, offer a strategic pathway for small enterprises to overcome these challenges. By empowering small businesses in the realm of cross-border transactions, Ripple contributes to a future where these vital economic players can actively participate in the international economic landscape. As we progress through subsequent chapters, we will further explore how Ripple's approach aligns with its broader mission of transforming the landscape of international transactions and fostering global financial inclusion.

Individuals find systems complex

In the intricate realm of cross-border payments, the complexity of systems can pose a significant challenge for individuals seeking to navigate international transactions. This chapter explores the specific hurdles faced by individuals in understanding and engaging with cross-border systems. From the intricacies of traditional correspondent banking to the lack of transparency, we delve into the reasons individuals find these systems complex. Additionally, we examine how Ripple's innovative solutions are strategically positioned to address these challenges, simplifying the cross-border payment landscape for individuals and fostering greater financial inclusion on a global scale.

Understanding the Complexity for Individuals:

The Nature of Cross-Border Systems: Cross-border payment systems, historically rooted in traditional correspondent banking models, often involve intricate processes and multiple intermediaries. The complexities arise from the need for coordination between financial institutions, currency conversion challenges, and compliance with regulatory requirements. Individuals engaging in international transactions may find these systems daunting and challenging to navigate.

Limited Transparency: A notable factor contributing to the complexity of cross-border systems is the limited transparency into the status and progress of transactions. Traditional correspondent banking models are known for their lack of real-time visibility, making it difficult for individuals to track the journey of their payments across multiple intermediaries. This opacity introduces uncertainties and erodes trust in the cross-border payment process.

Currency Exchange Challenges: The complexities associated with currency exchange add another layer of difficulty for individuals. Fluctuating exchange rates, additional fees for currency conversion, and the lack of standardized processes can make it challenging for individuals to understand the actual costs and outcomes of their cross-border transactions. This lack of clarity creates a barrier to informed decision-making.

Inadequate User-Friendly Interfaces: The interfaces through which individuals interact with cross-border payment systems can also contribute to the perceived complexity. In some cases, outdated or unintuitive platforms may hinder users from easily understanding the steps involved in initiating and tracking international transactions. This user experience challenge further intensifies the complexities individuals face.

Socio-Economic Impact on Individuals:

Frustration and Distrust: The complexity of cross-border systems can lead to frustration and a sense of distrust among individuals engaging in international transactions. When individuals encounter difficulties in understanding the status, fees, and timelines associated with their payments, it erodes confidence in the overall cross-border payment process. This frustration may discourage individuals from actively participating in cross-border transactions.

Impact on Remittance Recipients: Remittance recipients, often individuals reliant on timely and accurate fund transfers, bear the brunt of complex cross-border systems. Delays, additional fees, and uncertainties in the remittance process can impact the financial well-being of recipients. The lack of transparency into the status of remittances can create anxiety and financial stress for those awaiting funds from overseas.

Reduced Participation in Global Economy: Complex cross-border systems contribute to a scenario where individuals may be hesitant to participate in the global economy. The perceived difficulties in navigating international transactions may limit individuals' willingness to explore cross-border opportunities, such as online international shopping, global investments, or participation in the gig economy on a global scale.

Ripple's Approach to Simplifying Cross-Border Systems:

Real-Time Visibility and Transparency: One of Ripple's key strategies in simplifying cross-border systems is providing real-time visibility and transparency into the payment process. Through its decentralized and digital infrastructure, Ripple enables individuals to track the status of their transactions in real-time. This transparency fosters trust and empowers users with a clear understanding of the journey and progress of their payments.

Efficient Currency Conversion: Ripple's focus on efficient currency conversion addresses one of the core complexities for individuals in cross-border transactions. By utilizing the digital asset XRP as a bridge currency, Ripple facilitates swift and cost-effective currency conversion. This strategic use of digital assets minimizes the impact of fluctuating exchange rates, providing individuals with greater predictability and clarity on the costs associated with their transactions.

User-Friendly Interfaces: Ripple places a strong emphasis on creating user-friendly interfaces for individuals engaging in cross-border transactions. The platforms and applications powered by Ripple's technology are designed to be intuitive and accessible, reducing the learning curve for users. The aim is to provide individuals with a seamless and user-friendly experience, making it easier for them to initiate and track international payments.

Empowering Financial Institutions: Ripple's approach involves empowering financial institutions to enhance the user experience for individuals. By providing financial institutions with the tools and technology to offer streamlined cross-border payment services, Ripple contributes to creating a more user-centric approach. This empowerment extends to individuals, who can benefit from improved interfaces and processes offered by financial institutions leveraging Ripple's technology.

Empowering Individuals in Cross-Border Transactions:

Enhanced Control and Understanding: Ripple's focus on transparency and real-time visibility empowers individuals with enhanced control and understanding of their cross-border transactions. Users can track the progress of their payments, understand associated fees, and gain insights into the currency conversion process. This transparency enhances the overall user experience and reduces the perceived complexity of cross-border systems.

Cost-Effective Transactions: The efficient currency conversion facilitated by Ripple's technology contributes to more cost-effective transactions for individuals. By minimizing additional fees and providing a streamlined process for currency exchange, Ripple aims to make cross-border transactions more affordable and predictable. This cost-effectiveness encourages individuals to explore international opportunities without the fear of hidden or unpredictable costs.

Participation in Global Economy: Simplifying cross-border systems through Ripple's solutions creates an environment where individuals feel more confident and willing to participate in the global economy. The user-friendly interfaces, transparency, and efficiency provided by Ripple's technology remove barriers to entry, enabling individuals to explore and engage in international transactions with greater ease.

Conclusion: Navigating a Simplified Cross-Border Landscape:

The complexity of cross-border systems can be a significant hurdle for individuals seeking to engage in international transactions. Ripple's innovative solutions, driven by a commitment to transparency, efficient currency conversion, and user-friendly interfaces, are strategically positioned to address these challenges. By simplifying the cross-border payment landscape for individuals, Ripple contributes to a future where global financial transactions are accessible, transparent, and user-centric. As we progress through subsequent chapters, we will further explore how Ripple's approach aligns with its broader mission of transforming the landscape of international transactions and fostering global financial inclusion.

Chapter 4: The Opacity of International Transfers
Limited transparency into status

In the intricate landscape of cross-border payments, the opacity of international transfers is a significant pain point for individuals and businesses alike. This chapter delves into the specific challenges arising from the limited transparency into the status of international transfers. From the traditional correspondent banking model to the difficulties in tracking payments across multiple intermediaries, we explore the reasons behind the opacity. Additionally, we examine how Ripple's innovative solutions strategically address these challenges, providing a pathway for enhanced transparency and accountability in international transactions.

Understanding the Limited Transparency:

Traditional Correspondent Banking Model: The traditional correspondent banking model, which has been the backbone of cross-border transactions for decades, inherently lacks transparency. In this model, payments traverse through a series of intermediary banks before reaching the final destination. Each intermediary adds a layer of complexity, and the lack of a unified, real-time tracking mechanism makes it challenging for individuals and businesses to obtain timely and accurate information on the status of their international transfers.

Fragmented Information Flow: The information flow in cross-border transactions is often fragmented, with each intermediary holding partial information about the payment's journey. This fragmentation contributes to the limited transparency, as parties involved in the transaction struggle to access a comprehensive and real-time view of the payment's status. The lack of a standardized communication protocol further exacerbates this challenge.

Inherent Delays in Confirmation: Confirmation of payment status in traditional cross-border systems is subject to inherent delays. The time taken for messages to propagate through the correspondent banking network, coupled with manual processing at various stages, leads to delays in confirming the completion or status of a transaction. This delay can create uncertainty and erode trust in the international payment process.

Socio-Economic Impact of Limited Transparency:

Uncertainty in Business Transactions: Limited transparency into the status of international transfers introduces uncertainty into business transactions. Businesses engaged in cross-border trade may face challenges in confirming the receipt of payments or goods, leading to operational inefficiencies and potential disputes. This uncertainty can hinder the growth of international trade and negatively impact business relationships.

Challenges for Remittance Recipients: Remittance recipients, who often rely on timely and accurate fund transfers, bear the brunt of limited transparency. The inability to track the status of remittances in real-time can create anxiety and financial stress for recipients waiting for crucial funds. Delays or uncertainties in the confirmation of remittance status impact the financial well-being of individuals and families.

Compromised Financial Planning: Limited transparency disrupts individuals' and businesses' ability to plan and manage their finances effectively. The uncertainty surrounding the status of international transfers makes it challenging to predict when funds will be available or when transactions will be completed. This compromised financial planning can have cascading effects on various aspects of personal and business finances.

Ripple's Approach to Enhancing Transparency:

Real-Time Visibility through Decentralization: Ripple's approach to addressing the limited transparency in international transfers revolves around decentralization. By leveraging blockchain technology and a decentralized network, Ripple provides real-time visibility into the status of transactions. The decentralized nature of the network ensures that information is updated and accessible in a transparent manner, reducing the delays and uncertainties associated with traditional correspondent banking.

Immutable and Transparent Ledger: Ripple utilizes an immutable and transparent ledger, the XRP Ledger, to record and track transactions. This ledger is accessible to all participants in the network, allowing them to independently verify and confirm the status of transactions. The transparency provided by the XRP Ledger enhances accountability and instills confidence in the accuracy of transaction information.

Instant Settlements with On-Demand Liquidity (ODL): Ripple's On-Demand Liquidity (ODL) solution further contributes to enhanced transparency by enabling instant settlements. ODL utilizes the digital asset XRP as a bridge currency, facilitating real-time and cost-effective cross-border transactions. The instantaneous settlement eliminates the delays associated with traditional correspondent banking, providing users with immediate confirmation of the transaction status.

Unified Information Flow: Ripple's technology ensures a unified and standardized information flow in cross-border transactions. The use of a decentralized network and a transparent ledger eliminates the fragmentation of information, allowing all participants in the transaction to access a comprehensive and up-to-date view of the payment's status. This unified information flow reduces the complexities associated with tracking payments across multiple intermediaries.

Empowering Individuals and Businesses:

Enhanced Business Transaction Confidence: Ripple's focus on transparency empowers businesses engaged in cross-border trade by providing enhanced confidence in their transactions. Businesses can have real-time visibility into the status of payments, reducing uncertainties and facilitating smoother trade operations. The transparency offered by Ripple's solutions contributes to a more reliable and efficient international trade environment.

Improved Remittance Experience: For remittance recipients, Ripple's solutions create a more positive and predictable experience. The real-time visibility into the status of remittances ensures that recipients can track and confirm the receipt of funds promptly. This transparency enhances the overall remittance experience, alleviating anxiety and contributing to the financial well-being of individuals and families dependent on international transfers.

Optimized Financial Planning: The enhanced transparency provided by Ripple's technology allows individuals and businesses to optimize their financial planning. With real-time visibility into the status of international transfers, users can plan and manage their finances more effectively. The predictability offered by Ripple's solutions contributes to better financial decision-making and mitigates the challenges associated with compromised financial planning.

Conclusion: Towards a Transparent International Payment Landscape:

The limited transparency into the status of international transfers has been a longstanding challenge in the realm of cross-border payments. Ripple's innovative solutions, driven by a commitment to decentralization, transparent ledgers, instant settlements, and unified information flow, offer a strategic pathway to enhance transparency in international transactions. By providing real-time visibility and accountability, Ripple contributes to a future where individuals and businesses can engage in cross-border transactions with confidence and certainty. As we progress through subsequent chapters, we will further explore how Ripple's approach aligns with its broader mission of transforming the landscape of international transactions and fostering global financial inclusion.

Difficult to track payments across chains

In the intricate landscape of cross-border payments, the difficulty in tracking payments across chains stands out as a significant challenge. This chapter explores the specific hurdles arising from the fragmented nature of payment chains in international transactions. From the complexities of traditional correspondent banking to the lack of interoperability, we delve into the reasons tracking payments across multiple chains is a formidable task. Additionally, we examine how Ripple's innovative solutions strategically address these challenges, providing a pathway for seamless tracking and transparency in the cross-border payment ecosystem.

Understanding the Challenge of Tracking Across Chains:

Fragmentation in Traditional Correspondent Banking: Traditional correspondent banking models often involve a series of intermediary banks, each playing a role in facilitating the cross-border payment. The fragmented nature of these intermediaries creates a challenge in tracking payments seamlessly across the entire chain. Each bank may have its internal systems, processes, and timelines, leading to discrepancies and difficulties in maintaining a unified and transparent view of the payment's journey.

Lack of Standardization and Interoperability: The lack of standardization and interoperability in cross-border payment systems further complicates the tracking process. Different financial institutions may use disparate technologies, protocols, and messaging formats, making it challenging to establish a common ground for tracking payments. This lack of standardized communication protocols contributes to the opacity in understanding the status and progress of international transfers.

Inherent Delays and Information Gaps: As payments move across multiple chains in the correspondent banking network, inherent delays and information gaps emerge. The time taken for messages to traverse from one intermediary to another, coupled with manual processing at various stages, introduces delays in updating the status of payments. These delays create gaps in information flow, making it difficult to track payments in real-time.

Socio-Economic Impact of Tracking Challenges:

Operational Inefficiencies for Businesses: The difficulty in tracking payments across chains introduces operational inefficiencies for businesses engaged in cross-border trade. Businesses may struggle to reconcile and synchronize payment information from different intermediaries, leading to delays in confirming the completion of transactions. These operational inefficiencies can impact the overall efficiency and competitiveness of international trade operations.

Uncertainty for Remittance Recipients: Remittance recipients, reliant on timely and accurate fund transfers, face uncertainty when tracking payments across chains becomes challenging. Delays in the confirmation of payment status create anxiety for recipients awaiting crucial funds. The lack of real-time visibility into the progress of remittances can result in financial stress and uncertainty regarding when funds will be available.

Complicated Financial Record-Keeping: Individuals and businesses engaged in cross-border transactions often find it challenging to maintain accurate and consolidated financial records due to tracking difficulties. The fragmented nature of payment chains makes it complicated to compile and reconcile transaction information. This complicates financial record-keeping, hindering individuals and businesses from having a comprehensive view of their international financial activities.

Ripple's Approach to Seamless Tracking:

Blockchain Technology and Decentralization: Ripple's approach to addressing the difficulty in tracking payments across chains is grounded in the use of blockchain technology and decentralization. By leveraging a decentralized network and a transparent ledger, Ripple ensures that transaction information is recorded and updated in real-time. The blockchain's immutable nature guarantees that once a transaction is recorded, it cannot be altered, providing a reliable and unambiguous record of payment progress.

Unified Information Flow with the XRP Ledger: Ripple utilizes the XRP Ledger, an open-source blockchain, to establish a unified information flow in cross-border transactions. The XRP Ledger serves as a transparent and standardized record of transactions, accessible to all participants in the network. This unified information flow eliminates the fragmentation associated with traditional correspondent banking, allowing for seamless tracking across the entire payment chain.

Interledger Protocol (ILP) for Interoperability: Ripple's adoption of the Interledger Protocol (ILP) contributes to addressing the lack of interoperability in cross-border payments. ILP is designed to connect different payment networks, enabling interoperability between disparate systems. This protocol establishes a common framework for communication and settlement, facilitating the smooth movement of payments across various chains. Ripple's integration of ILP enhances the tracking capabilities of cross-border transactions.

Instant Settlements with On-Demand Liquidity (ODL): Ripple's On-Demand Liquidity (ODL) solution, powered by the digital asset XRP, plays a pivotal role in ensuring instant settlements and seamless tracking. ODL enables the use of XRP as a bridge currency, allowing for swift and cost-effective cross-border transactions. The instantaneous settlements provided by ODL eliminate delays and gaps in information flow, offering a real-time view of payment progress.

Empowering Businesses and Individuals:

Streamlined Trade Operations for Businesses: Ripple's focus on seamless tracking empowers businesses engaged in cross-border trade by streamlining their operations. The unified information flow and real-time visibility into payment progress contribute to operational efficiency. Businesses can reconcile and synchronize payment information more effectively, reducing the complexities associated with tracking payments across multiple chains.

Enhanced Remittance Experience for Recipients: For remittance recipients, Ripple's solutions create an enhanced and predictable experience. The real-time tracking capabilities ensure that recipients can monitor the progress of remittances and receive timely confirmation of fund availability. This transparency contributes to a positive remittance experience, alleviating uncertainty and financial stress for individuals awaiting crucial funds.

Simplified Financial Record-Keeping: Ripple's technology simplifies financial record-keeping for individuals and businesses engaged in cross-border transactions. The transparent and unified information flow provided by the XRP Ledger ensures that transaction records are easily accessible and verifiable. This simplification of financial record-keeping facilitates better financial management and decision-making.

Conclusion: Toward a Transparent and Interconnected Future:

The difficulty in tracking payments across chains has long been a challenge in cross-border payments. Ripple's innovative solutions, driven by blockchain technology, decentralization, interoperability, and instant settlements, offer a strategic pathway to address these challenges. By providing seamless tracking and transparency in the cross-border payment ecosystem, Ripple contributes to a future where businesses and individuals can engage in international transactions with confidence and clarity. As we progress through subsequent chapters, we will further explore how Ripple's approach aligns with its broader mission of transforming the landscape of international transactions and fostering global financial inclusion.

Errors and mismatches common

In the intricate realm of cross-border payments, the prevalence of errors and mismatches is a pervasive challenge that introduces complexity and uncertainty into the international financial landscape. This chapter delves into the specific hurdles arising from common errors and mismatches in international transfers. From the intricacies of traditional correspondent banking to the lack of standardized processes, we explore the reasons behind these issues. Additionally, we examine how Ripple's innovative solutions strategically address these challenges, providing a pathway for increased accuracy, efficiency, and transparency in cross-border payments.

Understanding the Prevalence of Errors and Mismatches:

Traditional Correspondent Banking Complexities: Traditional correspondent banking models are inherently complex, involving a series of intermediaries through which international payments must pass. At each stage, the potential for errors and mismatches increases due to manual processing, differing operational procedures, and fragmented communication. These complexities create a breeding ground for discrepancies that can have cascading effects on the accuracy of cross-border transactions.

Lack of Standardization: The lack of standardized processes in cross-border payments contributes significantly to errors and mismatches. Different financial institutions may employ distinct messaging formats, communication protocols, and transaction codes, leading to challenges in interpreting and reconciling information. This lack of standardization amplifies the risk of errors, as parties involved may interpret transaction details differently.

Currency Conversion Challenges: Currency conversion is a crucial aspect of cross-border payments, and discrepancies often arise due to fluctuations in exchange rates and additional fees. The lack of a standardized approach to currency conversion across different intermediaries can result in mismatches between the expected and actual amounts received. These discrepancies introduce uncertainties and complexities into the payment process.

Socio-Economic Impact of Errors and Mismatches:

Financial Losses for Businesses and Individuals: Errors and mismatches in cross-border payments can lead to financial losses for businesses and individuals. Discrepancies in transaction amounts, fees, or exchange rates may result in the underpayment or overpayment of funds. These financial losses not only impact the profitability of businesses but also create hardships for individuals who rely on accurate and timely fund transfers.

Operational Disruptions for Businesses: Businesses engaged in cross-border trade may face operational disruptions due to errors and mismatches. Reconciliation processes become more time-consuming and resource-intensive as discrepancies need to be identified and rectified. Operational disruptions can hinder the smooth flow of international trade, affecting supply chains and customer relationships.

Trust and Confidence Erosion: Errors and mismatches erode trust and confidence in the cross-border payment process. Parties involved in international transactions may become skeptical about the accuracy and reliability of the payment system. This erosion of trust can lead to strained relationships between businesses, financial institutions, and individuals engaged in cross-border transactions.

Ripple's Approach to Enhancing Accuracy and Efficiency:

Immutable and Transparent Ledger: Ripple's approach to addressing errors and mismatches is grounded in the use of blockchain technology and a transparent ledger. The XRP Ledger, Ripple's open-source blockchain, serves as an immutable and transparent record of transactions. Once a transaction is recorded, it cannot be altered, ensuring the accuracy and integrity of payment information. This transparency reduces the risk of errors and mismatches.

Real-Time Visibility and Tracking: Ripple's focus on real-time visibility contributes to the reduction of errors by providing instantaneous tracking of payments. Participants in the network can monitor the status and progress of transactions in real-time, enabling prompt identification and resolution of discrepancies. The real-time visibility enhances accuracy and minimizes the potential for errors to go unnoticed.

Interledger Protocol (ILP) for Standardization: Ripple's adoption of the Interledger Protocol (ILP) addresses the lack of standardization in cross-border payments. ILP serves as a common protocol for connecting different payment networks, facilitating standardized communication and settlement. The use of ILP contributes to a more uniform and standardized approach to cross-border transactions, reducing the likelihood of errors and mismatches.

On-Demand Liquidity (ODL) for Instant Settlements: Ripple's On-Demand Liquidity (ODL) solution, powered by the digital asset XRP, plays a crucial role in enhancing accuracy through instant settlements. ODL enables the use of XRP as a bridge currency, facilitating swift and cost-effective cross-border transactions with immediate settlement. The elimination of delays in settlement reduces the window for errors and ensures that transaction details align accurately.

Empowering Businesses and Individuals:

Efficient Reconciliation Processes for Businesses: Ripple's technology streamlines reconciliation processes for businesses engaged in cross-border trade. The transparent and immutable nature of the XRP Ledger ensures that transaction records are accurate and tamper-proof. This efficiency in reconciliation processes saves time and resources for businesses, allowing them to focus on core operations rather than resolving discrepancies.

Enhanced Financial Planning for Individuals: Individuals engaged in cross-border transactions benefit from Ripple's solutions through enhanced financial planning. The reduction of errors and mismatches provides individuals with greater confidence in the accuracy of their transactions. This, in turn, allows for more effective financial planning, as individuals can anticipate the expected amounts without the uncertainty introduced by discrepancies.

Strengthened Trust in Cross-Border Payments: Ripple's focus on accuracy and efficiency contributes to strengthening trust in the cross-border payment process. The transparent ledger, real-time visibility, and standardized protocols enhance the reliability of international transactions. Businesses, financial institutions, and individuals can engage in cross-border payments with increased confidence, knowing that the risk of errors and mismatches is significantly reduced.

Conclusion: A Pathway to Accurate and Reliable Cross-Border Transactions:

The prevalence of errors and mismatches in cross-border payments has long been a challenge that complicates international financial interactions. Ripple's innovative solutions, driven by blockchain technology, real-time visibility, standardization, and instant settlements, offer a strategic pathway to address these challenges. By providing increased accuracy, efficiency, and transparency in cross-border transactions, Ripple contributes to a future where businesses and individuals can engage in international financial activities with confidence and reliability. As we progress through subsequent chapters, we will further explore how Ripple's approach aligns with its broader mission of transforming the landscape of international transactions and fostering global financial inclusion.

Beneficiaries suffer from lack of clarity

In the intricate landscape of cross-border payments, the lack of clarity for beneficiaries emerges as a poignant challenge, impacting individuals and businesses awaiting international funds. This chapter explores the specific hurdles faced by beneficiaries due to the opacity in international transfers. From delays and uncertainties to the complexities of traditional correspondent banking, we delve into the reasons beneficiaries suffer from a lack of clarity. Additionally, we examine how Ripple's innovative solutions strategically address these challenges, providing a pathway for enhanced visibility, predictability, and empowerment for those awaiting crucial funds.

Understanding the Lack of Clarity for Beneficiaries:

Delays and Uncertainties in Traditional Models: Beneficiaries in cross-border payments often experience delays and uncertainties due to the traditional correspondent banking model's inherent complexities. As payments traverse through a series of intermediaries, each introducing potential delays, beneficiaries are left in the dark regarding the timing and certainty of fund availability. The lack of real-time updates contributes to a sense of uncertainty for individuals and businesses dependent on timely payments.

Opaque Tracking Mechanisms: The tracking mechanisms in traditional cross-border systems lack transparency, making it challenging for beneficiaries to monitor the progress of their payments. Beneficiaries may be unaware of the current status of the transaction, leading to anxieties and difficulties in financial planning. The opacity in tracking mechanisms further exacerbates the lack of clarity for those eagerly awaiting international funds.

Communication Gaps and Information Asymmetry: Communication gaps between the various intermediaries involved in cross-border payments contribute to information asymmetry. Beneficiaries may not have direct access to information about the transaction's progress, relying on outdated or limited communication from financial institutions. This lack of direct and real-time communication creates a gap in information flow, leaving beneficiaries uninformed about the status of their funds.

Socio-Economic Impact on Beneficiaries:

Financial Stress and Anxiety: The lack of clarity regarding the status of international transfers places beneficiaries under financial stress and anxiety. Individuals and businesses awaiting funds may face uncertainty about when the funds will be available, impacting their ability to meet financial obligations. The resulting stress can affect the overall well-being of beneficiaries, creating challenges in managing daily expenses and planning for the future.

Operational Disruptions for Businesses: Businesses dependent on timely cross-border payments may encounter operational disruptions due to a lack of clarity. The uncertainty surrounding fund availability can disrupt supply chains, hinder production processes, and strain relationships with suppliers and partners. These operational disruptions have a cascading effect on the overall efficiency and competitiveness of businesses engaged in international trade.

Impact on Remittance Recipients: Remittance recipients, often in need of timely funds for essential expenses, bear the brunt of the lack of clarity in international transfers. Delays and uncertainties in the arrival of remittance payments can lead to challenges in meeting immediate financial needs. The impact is particularly significant for recipients in developing regions who rely on remittances for daily living expenses and essential services.

Ripple's Approach to Enhancing Clarity for Beneficiaries:

Real-Time Visibility through Decentralization: Ripple's approach to addressing the lack of clarity for beneficiaries is grounded in decentralization and real-time visibility. By leveraging blockchain technology and a decentralized network, Ripple provides beneficiaries with real-time visibility into the status and progress of their international transfers. The decentralized nature of the network ensures that information is updated promptly, offering clarity and transparency to those awaiting funds.

Instant Settlements with On-Demand Liquidity (ODL): Ripple's On-Demand Liquidity (ODL) solution, powered by the digital asset XRP, plays a crucial role in enhancing clarity for beneficiaries through instant settlements. ODL enables the use of XRP as a bridge currency, facilitating immediate and cost-effective cross-border transactions. The instantaneous settlements ensure that beneficiaries receive prompt confirmation and clarity on the availability of funds, eliminating the uncertainties associated with traditional models.

Unified Information Flow with the XRP Ledger: Ripple utilizes the XRP Ledger, an open-source blockchain, to establish a unified information flow in cross-border transactions. The transparent and standardized record of transactions on the XRP Ledger ensures that beneficiaries have access to accurate and up-to-date information. This unified information flow reduces the complexities associated with tracking payments across multiple intermediaries, providing clarity for those awaiting funds.

Enhanced Communication Channels: Ripple's technology enhances communication channels between financial institutions and beneficiaries. Through user-friendly interfaces and streamlined communication protocols, beneficiaries can receive updates and notifications about the status of their international transfers. Improved communication channels contribute to reducing information gaps and ensuring that beneficiaries are well-informed throughout the payment process.

Empowering Beneficiaries in Cross-Border Transactions:

Confidence in Fund Availability: Ripple's focus on real-time visibility and instant settlements instills confidence in beneficiaries regarding the availability of funds. With immediate confirmation of the transaction's completion, beneficiaries can rely on accurate and up-to-date information about the arrival of funds. This confidence enhances financial planning and reduces the stress associated with uncertainties in fund availability.

Timely Meeting of Financial Needs: For remittance recipients and businesses awaiting cross-border payments, Ripple's solutions ensure the timely meeting of financial needs. The immediate settlements provided by ODL enable beneficiaries to access funds promptly, addressing immediate financial requirements. This timely access contributes to the well-being of individuals and the smooth operational flow for businesses.

Greater Control and Empowerment: Ripple's technology empowers beneficiaries by providing greater control over their cross-border transactions. With real-time visibility, beneficiaries can actively monitor the progress of their payments and receive instant notifications. This level of control enhances the overall user experience and empowers individuals and businesses to actively participate in international financial activities.

Conclusion: A Future of Clarity and Empowerment in Cross-Border Transactions:

The lack of clarity for beneficiaries in cross-border payments has long been a challenge, impacting individuals and businesses reliant on timely funds. Ripple's innovative solutions, driven by decentralization, real-time visibility, instant settlements, and enhanced communication channels, offer a strategic pathway to address these challenges. By providing clarity, transparency, and empowerment to those awaiting international funds, Ripple contributes to a future where cross-border transactions are seamless and predictable. As we progress through subsequent chapters, we will further explore how Ripple's approach aligns with its broader mission of transforming the landscape of international transactions and fostering global financial inclusion.

Chapter 5: The Need for Liquidity
Volatility in currency markets

In the dynamic world of cross-border payments, the need for liquidity stands out as a critical factor influencing the efficiency and cost-effectiveness of international transactions. This chapter explores the specific challenges arising from the volatility in currency markets, a key aspect contributing to the demand for enhanced liquidity. From the impact of currency fluctuations on transaction costs to the inefficiencies of pre-funded nostro accounts, we delve into the reasons behind the necessity for liquidity in the cross-border payment ecosystem. Additionally, we examine how Ripple's innovative solutions strategically address these challenges, providing a pathway for stability, cost reduction, and increased liquidity in international transactions.

Understanding Volatility in Currency Markets:

Currency Fluctuations and Exchange Rate Variability: Volatility in currency markets is characterized by fluctuations and variability in exchange rates. Currencies are subject to constant market forces influenced by economic indicators, geopolitical events, and market sentiment. The unpredictable nature of these factors results in currency values that can experience sudden and significant changes, introducing uncertainty into cross-border transactions.

Impact on Transaction Costs: The volatility in currency markets directly impacts transaction costs in cross-border payments. Fluctuations in exchange rates can lead to variations in the value of transactions, affecting the final amount received by beneficiaries. High volatility introduces risks for both individuals and businesses, as the cost of international transactions becomes less predictable, and unexpected changes in exchange rates can result in additional expenses.

Risk of Currency Devaluation and Depreciation: Currency markets are susceptible to the risk of devaluation or depreciation of currencies. Economic events, political instability, or changes in monetary policies can contribute to a decline in the value of a currency. For individuals and businesses engaging in cross-border transactions, the risk of currency devaluation poses challenges in accurately estimating the value of funds received, impacting financial planning and budgeting.

Socio-Economic Impact of Currency Volatility:

Uncertainty for Businesses Engaged in International Trade: Businesses involved in international trade face uncertainties due to currency volatility. Fluctuations in exchange rates introduce uncertainties in the cost of imported goods and services, affecting pricing strategies and profit margins. The lack of stability in currency values creates challenges for businesses to accurately forecast and manage the financial aspects of cross-border trade.

Financial Stress for Individuals and Remittance Recipients: Currency volatility contributes to financial stress for individuals and remittance recipients. Individuals relying on international remittances may experience variations in the value of received funds, impacting their ability to meet financial obligations. The unpredictability introduced by currency fluctuations adds an additional layer of uncertainty for those dependent on cross-border transactions for their livelihood.

Reduced Confidence in Cross-Border Transactions: Volatility in currency markets erodes confidence in the reliability and predictability of cross-border transactions. Both businesses and individuals may become hesitant to engage in international financial activities due to the potential risks associated with currency fluctuations. The reduced confidence further contributes to a reluctance to explore global opportunities and hinders the growth of international trade and financial inclusion.

Ripple's Approach to Addressing Currency Volatility:

Stability through XRP as a Bridge Currency: Ripple's approach to addressing currency volatility is grounded in the use of XRP as a bridge currency. XRP is a digital asset designed for rapid and cost-effective cross-border transactions. By leveraging XRP as a bridge currency in the On-Demand Liquidity (ODL) solution, Ripple introduces stability to cross-border transactions. XRP's quick settlement times minimize exposure to currency fluctuations, reducing the risk associated with volatile markets.

Real-Time Settlements and Minimization of Exposure: Ripple's On-Demand Liquidity facilitates real-time settlements using XRP, minimizing the exposure to currency volatility. Traditional cross-border systems often involve multi-day settlement periods, exposing transactions to potential fluctuations in exchange rates. Ripple's technology, with its focus on instant settlements, significantly reduces the window during which currency values can change, providing a level of stability and predictability.

Cost Reduction through Efficient Currency Conversion: Ripple's technology efficiently addresses currency volatility by reducing costs associated with currency conversion. The instantaneous nature of XRP settlements eliminates the need for pre-funding nostro accounts in multiple currencies, reducing the capital tied up in these accounts. This efficiency in currency conversion contributes to cost reduction and mitigates the impact of currency fluctuations on transaction expenses.

Empowering Businesses and Individuals with Stable Transactions:

Predictable Costs for Businesses: Ripple's focus on stability and efficient currency conversion empowers businesses engaged in international trade. The use of XRP as a bridge currency ensures that transactions are settled quickly and at a known cost, minimizing the impact of currency fluctuations on transaction expenses. This predictability allows businesses to confidently engage in cross-border trade with a clear understanding of the financial aspects involved.

Enhanced Financial Planning for Individuals and Remittance Recipients: For individuals and remittance recipients, Ripple's solutions contribute to enhanced financial planning by providing stability in cross-border transactions. The reduced exposure to currency volatility ensures that the value of received funds remains more predictable. This predictability allows individuals to plan their finances more effectively, alleviating the financial stress associated with unpredictable changes in currency values.

Increased Confidence in Cross-Border Transactions: Ripple's technology instills confidence in cross-border transactions by addressing currency volatility. The stability introduced through efficient currency conversion and real-time settlements enhances the overall reliability and predictability of international transactions. Businesses and individuals can engage in global financial activities with increased confidence, knowing that Ripple's solutions mitigate the risks associated with currency fluctuations.

Conclusion: Stability and Predictability in a Volatile World:

Currency volatility has long been a challenge in cross-border payments, introducing uncertainties and risks for businesses and individuals alike. Ripple's innovative solutions, driven by the use of XRP as a bridge currency, real-time settlements, and cost-efficient currency conversion, offer a strategic pathway to address the challenges posed by currency fluctuations. By providing stability, predictability, and cost reduction in international transactions, Ripple contributes to a future where businesses and individuals can engage in cross-border activities with confidence and resilience. As we progress through subsequent chapters, we will further explore how Ripple's approach aligns with its broader mission of transforming the landscape of international transactions and fostering global financial inclusion.

Pre-funded nostro accounts

In the intricate world of cross-border payments, the demand for liquidity is a central theme, crucial for the smooth and efficient functioning of international financial transactions. This chapter explores the specific challenges arising from pre-funded nostro accounts, a traditional model that has long been a cornerstone of cross-border payment systems. From the inefficiencies and capital requirements associated with pre-funding to the limitations of tied-up capital, we delve into the reasons behind the necessity for liquidity in the cross-border payment ecosystem. Additionally, we examine how Ripple's innovative solutions strategically address these challenges, providing a pathway for on-demand liquidity, cost reduction, and increased efficiency in international transactions.

Understanding Pre-funded Nostro Accounts:

The Traditional Correspondent Banking Model: Pre-funded nostro accounts are a fundamental component of the traditional correspondent banking model. In this model, financial institutions maintain accounts with each other in foreign currencies, known as nostro accounts. These accounts are pre-funded with a certain amount of capital to facilitate cross-border payments. The pre-funding requirement is based on the anticipation of future payment obligations, leading to the tie-up of significant amounts of capital across multiple currencies.

Capital Tied Up in Multiple Currencies: One of the primary challenges of pre-funded nostro accounts is the substantial amount of capital tied up in multiple currencies.

Financial institutions must allocate funds to these accounts to ensure they have sufficient liquidity for cross-border payments. This capital, spread across various currencies, is essentially immobilized, limiting its utility for other business purposes. The inefficiency of tying up capital in multiple nostro accounts represents a significant drawback of the traditional correspondent banking approach.

Risk and Inefficiency of Pre-funding: Pre-funding introduces risks and inefficiencies into cross-border payments. Financial institutions must estimate future payment obligations and pre-fund nostro accounts accordingly. However, these estimations may not align with the actual transaction volume, leading to either excess or insufficient pre-funding. Excess pre-funding ties up more capital than necessary, while insufficient pre-funding can result in delays and increased costs due to the need for additional capital to cover payment obligations.

Socio-Economic Impact of Pre-funded Nostro Accounts:

Reduced Capital Efficiency for Financial Institutions: Pre-funded nostro accounts limit the capital efficiency of financial institutions. The capital allocated to these accounts could otherwise be utilized for investment, lending, or other revenue-generating activities. The reduced efficiency of capital utilization negatively impacts the overall financial performance of institutions engaged in cross-border transactions.

Increased Costs Passed On to Customers: The inefficiencies associated with pre-funded nostro accounts contribute to increased costs in cross-border payments. Financial institutions, grappling with the tie-up of capital and the risk of inaccurate pre-funding estimations, often pass on these costs to customers. The end result is higher fees for individuals and businesses engaged in international transactions, making cross-border payments less cost-effective.

Limitations on Financial Inclusion: Pre-funded nostro accounts pose limitations on financial inclusion, particularly in regions with smaller financial institutions. The capital requirements and operational complexities associated with maintaining nostro accounts can be prohibitive for smaller players, restricting their ability to participate in cross-border transactions. This limitation impedes global financial inclusion efforts and hinders access to international markets for smaller financial institutions.

Ripple's Approach to Addressing Pre-funded Nostro Accounts:

On-Demand Liquidity (ODL) and XRP as a Bridge Currency: Ripple's approach to addressing the challenges of pre-funded nostro accounts is centered around the use of On-Demand Liquidity (ODL) and XRP as a bridge currency. ODL enables real-time, cost-effective cross-border transactions by utilizing the digital asset XRP as a bridge between different fiat currencies. Rather than maintaining pre-funded nostro accounts, financial institutions can leverage XRP for instant and on-demand liquidity, eliminating the need for excess capital tied up in multiple currencies.

Efficient Utilization of Capital: Ripple's technology enhances the efficiency of capital utilization for financial institutions. With ODL, institutions can avoid the excessive tie-up of capital in pre-funded nostro accounts. The use of XRP as a bridge currency allows for the instant conversion of funds, minimizing the need for large amounts of pre-funded capital. This efficient utilization of capital contributes to improved financial performance and flexibility for institutions engaged in cross-border transactions.

Mitigating Risk through On-Demand Liquidity: Ripple's ODL solution mitigates the risks associated with inaccurate pre-funding estimations. The real-time nature of transactions using XRP ensures that financial institutions only need to hold sufficient XRP for immediate settlement. This eliminates the risk of excess or insufficient pre-funding, reducing the potential for delays and the associated costs. The risk mitigation aspect enhances the reliability and predictability of cross-border payments.

Empowering Financial Institutions and Promoting Inclusion:

Enhanced Profitability and Competitiveness: Ripple's technology empowers financial institutions by enhancing profitability and competitiveness in the cross-border payments landscape. The elimination of the pre-funded nostro account model reduces the capital constraints faced by institutions, allowing for more efficient use of resources. This, in turn, enhances the overall profitability and competitiveness of financial institutions engaged in international transactions.

Cost Reduction Passed On to Customers: Ripple's approach to on-demand liquidity translates into cost reduction, benefiting end-users of cross-border payment services.

Financial institutions, freed from the constraints of maintaining pre-funded nostro accounts, can pass on the cost savings to their customers. Reduced fees make cross-border transactions more affordable for individuals and businesses, aligning with Ripple's vision of fostering a more inclusive and accessible global financial system.

Enabling Participation of Smaller Financial Institutions: Ripple's technology facilitates the participation of smaller financial institutions in cross-border transactions. By removing the need for extensive capital tied up in nostro accounts, Ripple's solutions lower the barriers to entry for smaller players. This inclusivity promotes the participation of a diverse range of financial institutions, fostering a more interconnected and accessible global financial network.

Conclusion: Unleashing Liquidity and Efficiency in Cross-Border Transactions:

The inefficiencies and limitations posed by pre-funded nostro accounts have long been inherent in traditional cross-border payment models. Ripple's innovative solutions, driven by the use of On-Demand Liquidity and XRP as a bridge currency, offer a transformative pathway to address these challenges. By eliminating the need for excessive capital tied up in multiple currencies, Ripple contributes to increased efficiency, cost reduction, and enhanced liquidity in cross-border transactions. As we progress through subsequent chapters, we will further explore how Ripple's approach aligns with its broader mission of transforming the landscape of international transactions and fostering global financial inclusion.

Captured capital that could be deployed

In the complex ecosystem of cross-border payments, the demand for liquidity is a pivotal aspect shaping the efficiency and effectiveness of international financial transactions. This chapter explores the specific challenges associated with captured capital, a phenomenon where funds are immobilized in traditional models, limiting their deployment for more productive uses. From the impact of tied-up capital on financial institutions to the opportunity cost of immobilized funds, we delve into the reasons behind the necessity for liquidity in the cross-border payment landscape. Additionally, we examine how Ripple's innovative solutions strategically address these challenges, providing a pathway for liberated capital, increased operational flexibility, and a more dynamic global financial system.

Understanding Captured Capital:

Immobilized Funds in Traditional Models: Captured capital refers to the funds immobilized or tied up in various stages of the traditional cross-border payment process. In the conventional correspondent banking model, financial institutions are required to maintain pre-funded nostro accounts, tying up significant amounts of capital in multiple currencies. This immobilization of funds restricts their use for other purposes, limiting the overall flexibility and efficiency of capital utilization.

Opportunity Cost of Tied-Up Capital: The concept of captured capital introduces the notion of opportunity cost, representing the potential benefits that financial institutions forego by immobilizing funds. Tied-up capital in pre-funded nostro accounts could otherwise be deployed for investments, lending, or other revenue-generating activities. The opportunity cost incurred due to captured capital represents a missed opportunity for financial institutions to enhance their profitability and operational flexibility.

Operational Inefficiencies in the Traditional Model: Captured capital contributes to operational inefficiencies in the traditional cross-border payment model. The need to maintain pre-funded nostro accounts results in complex liquidity management processes, with financial institutions dedicating resources to managing and reconciling these accounts. This operational overhead adds to the overall inefficiency of the traditional model, hindering the agility and responsiveness of financial institutions.

Socio-Economic Impact of Captured Capital:

Reduced Capital Flexibility for Financial Institutions: Captured capital reduces the flexibility of financial institutions to deploy funds according to their strategic priorities. The tie-up of capital in pre-funded nostro accounts limits the ability of institutions to respond dynamically to changing market conditions, investment opportunities, or emerging business needs. This reduced flexibility hampers the overall adaptability of financial institutions in the rapidly evolving global financial landscape.

Impact on Profitability and Return on Assets (ROA): The immobilization of funds has a direct impact on the profitability of financial institutions. Captured capital represents a static component that generates limited returns compared to actively deployed assets. Financial institutions, constrained by the need to maintain pre-funded nostro accounts, may experience diminished returns on assets, affecting their overall profitability and financial performance.

Restricted Capacity for Innovation and Growth: The opportunity cost associated with captured capital restricts the capacity of financial institutions for innovation and growth. The funds tied up in traditional models could otherwise be allocated to strategic initiatives, technology upgrades, or expansion into new markets. The limitations imposed by captured capital hinder the ability of institutions to innovate and pursue growth opportunities, potentially impeding their competitiveness in the global financial landscape.

Ripple's Approach to Liberating Captured Capital:

On-Demand Liquidity (ODL) for Real-Time Liquidity: Ripple's approach to addressing captured capital is anchored in the use of On-Demand Liquidity (ODL), a solution designed to provide real-time liquidity through the digital asset XRP. ODL eliminates the need for pre-funded nostro accounts by leveraging XRP as a bridge currency. Financial institutions can source liquidity in real-time, reducing the immobilization of capital and liberating funds for immediate use in cross-border transactions.

Dynamic Utilization of Liquidity with XRP: Ripple's technology enables the dynamic utilization of liquidity through the efficient use of XRP. Instead of maintaining static pre-funded nostro accounts, financial institutions can access XRP on-demand, instantly converting one currency into another for cross-border settlements. This dynamic approach allows for the efficient deployment of liquidity precisely when needed, minimizing the opportunity cost associated with captured capital.

Cost Reduction and Increased Operational Efficiency: The adoption of Ripple's solutions leads to cost reduction and increased operational efficiency for financial institutions. By eliminating the need for pre-funded nostro accounts, institutions can streamline their liquidity management processes. The reduction in operational overhead and the elimination of reconciliation efforts contribute to a more efficient and agile operational framework.

Empowering Financial Institutions for Growth:

Enhanced Profitability and Return on Assets: Ripple's technology empowers financial institutions by enhancing profitability and optimizing return on assets. With the liberation of captured capital through ODL, institutions can redirect funds towards revenue-generating activities, investments, and strategic initiatives. This enhanced flexibility allows for a more dynamic allocation of resources, leading to improved returns on assets and overall financial performance.

Strategic Innovation and Market Expansion: The liberation of captured capital positions financial institutions to pursue strategic innovation and market expansion. Freed from the constraints of immobilized funds, institutions can allocate resources to technological advancements, product development, and expansion into new geographical markets.

This strategic flexibility fosters innovation and enables institutions to explore growth opportunities in the ever-evolving global financial landscape.

Resilience and Competitiveness in the Industry: Ripple's approach empowers financial institutions to build resilience and maintain competitiveness in the face of market dynamics. The liberated capital allows institutions to adapt swiftly to changing conditions, respond to emerging trends, and stay ahead of competitors. The ability to dynamically deploy liquidity positions institutions as more resilient and agile players in the competitive cross-border payments landscape.

Conclusion: Unleashing Capital for a Dynamic Future:

Captured capital, a longstanding challenge in traditional cross-border payment models, restricts the flexibility and potential growth of financial institutions. Ripple's innovative solutions, driven by the use of On-Demand Liquidity and XRP as a bridge currency, offer a transformative pathway to liberate capital from pre-funded nostro accounts. By providing real-time liquidity, reducing operational inefficiencies, and empowering financial institutions to deploy funds dynamically, Ripple contributes to a more dynamic and responsive global financial system. As we progress through subsequent chapters, we will further explore how Ripple's approach aligns with its broader mission of transforming the landscape of international transactions and fostering global financial inclusion.

Low liquidity increases costs

In the intricate realm of cross-border payments, the demand for liquidity plays a pivotal role in determining the efficiency and cost-effectiveness of international financial transactions. This chapter explores the specific challenges posed by low liquidity, a condition that can substantially increase costs and hinder the smooth flow of funds across borders. From the impact of illiquidity on transaction speed to the inefficiencies in managing liquidity buffers, we delve into the reasons behind the necessity for adequate liquidity in the cross-border payment landscape. Additionally, we examine how Ripple's innovative solutions strategically address these challenges, providing a pathway for enhanced liquidity, reduced costs, and increased operational efficiency in international transactions.

Understanding the Impact of Low Liquidity:

Transaction Speed and Settlement Delays: Low liquidity in cross-border payment corridors has a direct impact on transaction speed and settlement times. Illiquid markets can result in delays as financial institutions struggle to find counterparties willing to facilitate the necessary currency conversions. The lack of available liquidity hinders the swift execution of transactions, leading to prolonged settlement times and potential disruptions in the flow of funds.

Increased Transaction Costs: One of the primary consequences of low liquidity is the escalation of transaction costs. In illiquid markets, financial institutions may face challenges in obtaining favorable exchange rates, leading to increased costs for currency conversion. Additionally, the limited availability of liquidity may compel institutions to use alternative, more expensive liquidity sources, further contributing to elevated transaction expenses.

Managing Liquidity Buffers and Costs: Financial institutions often maintain liquidity buffers to address fluctuations in transaction volumes and market conditions. In the context of low liquidity, managing these buffers becomes a challenging task. Institutions may need to allocate more capital to maintain sufficient liquidity, incurring additional costs. The inefficiencies in managing liquidity buffers in illiquid markets contribute to the overall complexity and expense of cross-border payments.

Socio-Economic Impact of Low Liquidity:

Reduced Access to Financial Services: Low liquidity in cross-border payment corridors can lead to reduced access to financial services, particularly in regions with underdeveloped financial infrastructure. The challenges of sourcing liquidity in illiquid markets may deter financial institutions from offering services in certain regions, limiting access to international transactions for businesses and individuals in those areas.

Impact on Remittances and Financial Inclusion: Remittance recipients, often in need of timely and cost-effective fund transfers, are disproportionately affected by low liquidity. Delays and increased costs associated with illiquid corridors can hinder the accessibility of remittance services. This impact is particularly pronounced in regions where remittances play a crucial role in supporting the financial well-being of individuals and families, contributing to financial exclusion.

Disincentive for International Trade: Low liquidity acts as a disincentive for international trade, affecting businesses engaged in cross-border transactions. The increased costs and uncertainties associated with illiquid markets can discourage businesses from exploring global markets, hindering economic growth and limiting the potential for international trade partnerships.

Ripple's Approach to Enhancing Liquidity:

On-Demand Liquidity (ODL) for Real-Time Settlements: Ripple's innovative approach to addressing the challenges of low liquidity is anchored in the use of On-Demand Liquidity (ODL). ODL leverages the digital asset XRP as a bridge currency, enabling real-time settlements for cross-border transactions. By facilitating instant and cost-effective currency conversions through XRP, Ripple's technology eliminates the delays and increased costs associated with low liquidity in traditional models.

Efficient Use of XRP to Minimize Costs: Ripple's technology promotes the efficient use of XRP as a bridge currency to minimize costs in cross-border transactions. In illiquid corridors, the quick and direct conversion of funds using XRP reduces the reliance on multiple intermediaries and expensive liquidity sources. The efficient use of XRP as a liquidity solution contributes to cost reduction, making cross-border payments more affordable for financial institutions and end-users.

Enhanced Liquidity and Market Accessibility: Ripple's solutions contribute to enhanced liquidity and market accessibility by providing a reliable source of on-demand liquidity. Financial institutions connected to the Ripple network can tap into the liquidity available through XRP, facilitating smoother and faster cross-border transactions. This enhanced liquidity fosters market accessibility, particularly in regions that may face challenges in sourcing liquidity through traditional means.

Empowering Financial Inclusion and Global Trade:

Improved Access to Financial Services: Ripple's technology improves access to financial services by addressing the challenges of low liquidity. The availability of on-demand liquidity through XRP enables financial institutions to offer more accessible and cost-effective cross-border payment services. This improved access benefits businesses and individuals in regions that were previously underserved due to liquidity constraints, contributing to greater financial inclusion.

Efficient Remittance Services: Ripple's approach enhances the efficiency of remittance services by mitigating the impact of low liquidity. The real-time settlements facilitated by ODL reduce delays and costs associated with remittances, making these services more attractive and accessible. This efficiency is particularly beneficial for individuals and families reliant on timely remittance payments for their financial well-being.

Stimulating International Trade: Ripple's technology serves as a catalyst for international trade by overcoming the challenges posed by low liquidity. The reduction in transaction costs, swift settlements, and enhanced liquidity availability create a more favorable environment for businesses engaged in cross-border trade. The stimulation of international trade contributes to economic growth, job creation, and increased opportunities for businesses on a global scale.

Conclusion: Navigating the Waters of Cross-Border Transactions with Adequate Liquidity:

Low liquidity has long been a stumbling block in the world of cross-border payments, introducing delays, increasing costs, and limiting access to financial services. Ripple's innovative solutions, driven by the use of On-Demand Liquidity and XRP as a bridge currency, offer a transformative pathway to enhance liquidity, reduce costs, and foster a more efficient global financial system. By addressing the challenges associated with low liquidity, Ripple contributes to a future where cross-border transactions are swift, cost-effective, and accessible to businesses and individuals around the world. As we progress through subsequent chapters, we will further explore how Ripple's approach aligns with its broader mission of transforming the landscape of international transactions and fostering global financial inclusion.

Chapter 6: The Interoperability Challenge
Disconnected payment silos

In the intricate landscape of cross-border payments, interoperability stands out as a critical factor determining the efficiency and seamlessness of international financial transactions. This chapter delves into the specific challenges posed by disconnected payment silos, a prevalent issue where different payment systems operate in isolation, hindering the flow of information and funds across diverse networks. From the impact on transaction speed to the complexities of reconciling disparate systems, we explore the reasons behind the necessity for enhanced interoperability in the cross-border payment ecosystem. Additionally, we examine how Ripple's innovative solutions strategically address these challenges, providing a pathway for connected payment networks, increased efficiency, and a more cohesive global financial system.

Understanding Disconnected Payment Silos:

Fragmentation in Payment Systems: Disconnected payment silos refer to the fragmentation and lack of cohesion among different payment systems operating globally. In the traditional cross-border payment landscape, various financial institutions and service providers utilize proprietary systems that are often incompatible with one another. This fragmentation leads to isolated payment silos, where information and funds are confined within distinct networks, creating barriers to seamless interoperability.

Limited Communication between Systems: One of the primary challenges posed by disconnected payment silos is the limited communication between different systems. Each payment network may have its own set of protocols, standards, and formats for transaction data, making it challenging for these systems to exchange information effectively. The lack of standardized communication hampers the interoperability between payment networks, resulting in delays and inefficiencies in cross-border transactions.

Complex Reconciliation Processes: The presence of disconnected payment silos complicates the reconciliation processes involved in cross-border transactions. When funds move between different payment systems, the lack of standardized communication often requires manual intervention to reconcile transaction data. This manual reconciliation introduces operational inefficiencies, increases the risk of errors, and contributes to delays in confirming the status of cross-border payments.

Socio-Economic Impact of Disconnected Payment Silos:

Impact on Transaction Speed: Disconnected payment silos have a direct impact on transaction speed in cross-border payments. The lack of interoperability between different systems introduces additional steps and processes to facilitate transactions across networks. The need for manual interventions and complex reconciliation further extends the time required for cross-border payments to be completed, affecting the overall speed and responsiveness of the financial system.

Increased Costs and Inefficiencies: The presence of disconnected payment silos contributes to increased costs and operational inefficiencies in cross-border transactions. The manual reconciliation processes, additional layers of communication, and the lack of standardized protocols result in higher operational expenses for financial institutions. These increased costs are often passed on to end-users, making cross-border payments less cost-effective.

Limited Accessibility and Financial Inclusion: Disconnected payment silos can limit accessibility to cross-border financial services, particularly in regions with underdeveloped financial infrastructure. The lack of interoperability may deter financial institutions from extending their services to certain areas, contributing to financial exclusion. This limitation hampers efforts to enhance global financial inclusion and restricts access to international transactions for businesses and individuals in underserved regions.

Ripple's Approach to Connected Payment Networks:

Interledger Protocol (ILP) for Seamless Interoperability: Ripple's innovative approach to addressing disconnected payment silos is grounded in the use of the Interledger Protocol (ILP). ILP is an open standard designed to facilitate seamless interoperability between different payment networks. By providing a protocol for connecting disparate ledgers, ILP enables the efficient exchange of information and funds across diverse payment systems, overcoming the challenges posed by disconnected silos.

Standardized Communication for Efficiency: Ripple's solutions prioritize standardized communication through ILP to enhance efficiency in cross-border transactions. ILP establishes a common language for different payment networks, allowing them to communicate and exchange information in a standardized format. This standardized communication streamlines the flow of transaction data, reducing the need for manual interventions and enhancing the overall efficiency of cross-border payments.

Reduced Reconciliation Efforts with ILP: The implementation of ILP significantly reduces the reconciliation efforts associated with cross-border transactions. By enabling seamless communication between different payment networks, ILP minimizes the need for manual reconciliation processes. This reduction in reconciliation efforts enhances the speed of cross-border transactions and contributes to a more streamlined and error-resistant financial ecosystem.

Empowering Global Financial Inclusion:

Enhanced Transaction Speed for Accessibility: Ripple's approach to connected payment networks enhances transaction speed, contributing to greater accessibility to cross-border financial services. The efficient exchange of information and funds facilitated by ILP reduces the time required for transactions to be completed. This enhanced speed is particularly beneficial for businesses and individuals in regions where timely access to cross-border payments is crucial for financial well-being.

Cost Reduction and Improved Affordability: Ripple's solutions, driven by ILP, contribute to cost reduction and improved affordability in cross-border transactions. The streamlined communication and reduced reconciliation efforts translate into operational efficiencies for financial institutions. The cost savings achieved through these efficiencies can be passed on to end-users, making cross-border payments more affordable and aligning with Ripple's vision of fostering an inclusive global financial system.

Expanding Access to Underserved Regions: Connected payment networks, facilitated by ILP, contribute to the expansion of financial services in underserved regions. The interoperability provided by ILP enables financial institutions to extend their networks and services to areas that were previously excluded due to the challenges of disconnected payment silos. This expansion supports global financial inclusion efforts, bringing cross-border financial services to a more diverse range of businesses and individuals.

Conclusion: Bridging the Divide with Connected Payment Networks:

Disconnected payment silos have long been a hurdle in the seamless flow of funds and information across borders. Ripple's innovative solutions, leveraging the Interledger Protocol, offer a transformative pathway to address the challenges of interoperability. By connecting payment networks and establishing standardized communication through ILP, Ripple contributes to a future where cross-border transactions are efficient, cost-effective, and accessible to a broader global audience. As we progress through subsequent chapters, we will further explore how Ripple's approach aligns with its broader mission of transforming the landscape of international transactions and fostering global financial inclusion.

Lack of standardization

In the ever-evolving realm of cross-border payments, the pursuit of interoperability remains a central theme. This chapter explores a significant impediment to seamless connectivity: the lack of standardization. Within this context, we delve into the complexities arising from disparate standards, protocols, and formats in the global payment landscape. The absence of uniformity poses challenges to communication and collaboration between different payment systems, hindering the realization of a fully interoperable cross-border payment ecosystem. Additionally, we will examine how Ripple's innovative solutions, specifically its focus on standardization through the Interledger Protocol (ILP), strategically address these challenges, paving the way for greater cohesion, efficiency, and interconnectedness within the global financial system.

Understanding the Lack of Standardization:

Fragmented Standards and Protocols: The lack of standardization in cross-border payments manifests through the existence of fragmented standards and protocols. Different financial institutions and payment networks often operate with their proprietary standards, making it challenging to establish a common ground for communication. This fragmentation results in a multitude of standards and protocols that coexist but do not seamlessly interact, leading to inefficiencies in cross-border transactions.

Format Divergence in Transaction Data: Another aspect of the lack of standardization is the divergence in the formats of transaction data. Each payment system may use its own set of data formats, making it difficult for these systems to interpret and process information consistently. The absence of a standardized format for transaction data introduces complexities in exchanging information between disparate payment networks, contributing to delays and potential errors in cross-border transactions.

Incompatibility of Messaging Protocols: In addition to format divergence, the lack of standardization extends to the messaging protocols used by different payment systems. Messaging protocols serve as the language through which systems communicate, and the incompatibility of these protocols creates barriers to effective communication. The inability of systems to understand and interpret messages from other networks further exacerbates the challenges of achieving interoperability.

Socio-Economic Impact of the Lack of Standardization:

Operational Inefficiencies and Increased Costs: The lack of standardization introduces operational inefficiencies in cross-border payments, leading to increased costs for financial institutions. The need to navigate diverse standards and protocols complicates the integration of different payment systems. Financial institutions must invest resources in developing and maintaining interfaces that can interpret and process information according to various standards, contributing to higher operational expenses.

Delays in Transaction Processing: The absence of standardized communication and data formats contributes to delays in transaction processing. In a landscape where speed is crucial, especially for cross-border transactions, the inability of different systems to seamlessly understand and process information hampers the efficiency of the entire payment ecosystem. These delays can have implications for businesses and individuals relying on timely transactions for various financial activities.

Reduced Accessibility and Financial Inclusion: The lack of standardization can limit accessibility to cross-border financial services, particularly in regions with underdeveloped financial infrastructure. Financial institutions may be hesitant to extend their services to areas where the absence of standardization complicates integration. This limitation hinders efforts to enhance global financial inclusion, leaving certain regions underserved in terms of international financial transactions.

Ripple's Approach to Standardization through ILP:

Interledger Protocol (ILP) as a Unifying Standard: Ripple's innovative approach to addressing the lack of standardization is anchored in the use of the Interledger Protocol (ILP). ILP serves as a unifying standard designed to establish a common language for different payment networks. By providing a standardized framework for communication and the exchange of transaction data, ILP mitigates the challenges arising from the lack of standardization in the cross-border payment landscape.

Common Language for Transaction Data: ILP introduces a common language for transaction data, addressing the format divergence that often plagues cross-border payments. Through ILP, different payment systems can communicate using a standardized format, ensuring that transaction data is universally understood and processed. This common language simplifies the integration of disparate systems, reducing the complexity and costs associated with navigating diverse data formats.

Facilitating Interoperability through ILP: Ripple's focus on standardization through ILP facilitates interoperability between different payment networks. ILP serves as a bridge that allows funds to flow seamlessly across disparate ledgers, overcoming the challenges posed by incompatible messaging protocols. This interoperability is essential for creating a more connected and cohesive cross-border payment ecosystem.

Empowering Global Financial Inclusion:

Operational Efficiencies and Cost Reduction: Ripple's emphasis on standardization contributes to operational efficiencies and cost reduction for financial institutions. With ILP providing a common language for transaction data, institutions can streamline their integration processes. The reduced complexity in interpreting and processing information leads to lower operational expenses, enabling financial institutions to offer more cost-effective cross-border payment services.

Swift and Predictable Transaction Processing: Standardization through ILP enhances the speed and predictability of transaction processing in cross-border payments. The common language established by ILP ensures that transaction data is swiftly and accurately interpreted by different payment networks. This swift processing is particularly crucial for businesses and individuals who rely on timely cross-border transactions for various financial activities.

Expanding Access to Underserved Regions: Ripple's commitment to standardization fosters the expansion of financial services in underserved regions. The simplified integration facilitated by ILP enables financial institutions to extend their networks to areas that were previously excluded due to the complexities of diverse standards. This expansion supports global financial inclusion efforts, bringing cross-border financial services to a more diverse range of businesses and individuals.

Conclusion: Forging a Common Path with Standardization:

The lack of standardization has posed significant challenges in the quest for interoperability in cross-border payments. Ripple's innovative solutions, centered around the Interledger Protocol, offer a transformative pathway to address these challenges. By establishing a common language for transaction data and facilitating interoperability between disparate payment networks, Ripple contributes to a future where cross-border transactions are more efficient, cost-effective, and accessible to a broader global audience. As we progress through subsequent chapters, we will further explore how Ripple's approach aligns with its broader mission of transforming the landscape of international transactions and fostering global financial inclusion.

Partnerships required between systems

In the intricate web of cross-border payments, achieving seamless interoperability is a multifaceted challenge. One significant aspect contributing to this challenge is the necessity for partnerships between different payment systems. This chapter explores the complexities arising from the requirement for collaboration and coordination between diverse systems, each operating with its unique infrastructure, protocols, and stakeholders. The demand for partnerships reflects the interdependent nature of the global financial ecosystem, where the ability of different systems to work in tandem is crucial for the efficient and interconnected flow of funds. Additionally, we will examine how Ripple's innovative solutions strategically address the challenges of fostering partnerships, paving the way for enhanced collaboration, and a more cohesive global financial system.

Navigating the Landscape of Partnerships:

Interconnected yet Disparate Systems: The landscape of cross-border payments is characterized by a multitude of interconnected yet disparate systems. Financial institutions, payment networks, and service providers each operate within their own infrastructure, often with unique protocols and standards. Achieving interoperability in such a diverse environment requires forging partnerships that enable these systems to communicate and collaborate effectively.

Coordination Across Ecosystems: The need for partnerships arises from the requirement for coordination across different ecosystems within the global financial landscape. Financial institutions may be part of diverse networks, each with its specific strengths and capabilities. To facilitate seamless cross-border transactions, these ecosystems must coordinate and collaborate, necessitating partnerships that transcend organizational boundaries.

Stakeholder Alignment and Collaboration: Partnerships are not only about the integration of technical systems but also about aligning the interests and goals of diverse stakeholders. Achieving interoperability requires collaboration not only between systems but also between the various entities involved, including banks, regulators, technology providers, and end-users. Building partnerships that foster stakeholder alignment is crucial for creating a cohesive and efficient cross-border payment ecosystem.

Socio-Economic Impact of Partnerships:

Operational Synergy and Efficiency Gains: Partnerships between different payment systems contribute to operational synergy and efficiency gains. By aligning technical infrastructure and coordinating processes, financial institutions can reduce redundancy and streamline operations. This operational synergy translates into efficiency gains, allowing for quicker and more cost-effective cross-border transactions.

Enhanced Speed and Responsiveness: Collaborative partnerships enable enhanced speed and responsiveness in cross-border payments. Through seamless coordination, information can be exchanged swiftly between systems, reducing the time required for transaction processing. This increased speed is particularly crucial in a global financial ecosystem where delays can have implications for businesses, individuals, and the overall efficiency of the financial system.

Reduced Costs Through Economies of Scale: Partnerships contribute to reduced costs through economies of scale. Collaborative efforts allow financial institutions to share resources, technology infrastructure, and operational processes, leading to cost savings. This reduction in costs can be passed on to end-users, making cross-border payments more affordable and aligning with the goal of fostering financial inclusion.

Ripple's Approach to Facilitating Partnerships:

Interledger Protocol (ILP) as a Catalyst for Collaboration: Ripple's innovative approach to addressing the need for partnerships is grounded in the use of the Interledger Protocol (ILP). ILP serves as a catalyst for collaboration by providing a standardized framework that enables different payment systems to interconnect. ILP facilitates partnerships by allowing systems to exchange information and value seamlessly, irrespective of their individual technical specifications.

Unified Framework for Stakeholder Alignment: ILP goes beyond technical integration and serves as a unified framework for stakeholder alignment. Financial institutions, regulators, technology providers, and other stakeholders can align their interests within the common language provided by ILP. This alignment fosters a collaborative environment where diverse entities can work together towards common goals, overcoming the challenges of fragmented ecosystems.

Building a Network of Connected Systems: Ripple's focus on partnerships extends to building a network of connected systems through ILP. Financial institutions connected to the Ripple network can seamlessly transact with each other, creating a network effect that enhances the overall efficiency of cross-border payments. This interconnected network serves as a model for how partnerships can be leveraged to overcome the challenges of interoperability.

Empowering Global Financial Inclusion:

Extending Financial Services Through Collaboration: Partnerships play a crucial role in extending financial services to underserved regions. Collaborative efforts between financial institutions enable the expansion of cross-border payment services to areas that were previously excluded. This extension of services contributes to global financial inclusion, ensuring that a broader spectrum of businesses and individuals can participate in the global economy.

Supporting Regulatory Alignment: Partnerships also support regulatory alignment, a critical aspect of achieving interoperability in cross-border payments. By collaborating with regulators and other stakeholders, financial institutions can navigate regulatory complexities and ensure compliance with diverse legal frameworks. Regulatory alignment through partnerships creates a conducive environment for efficient and compliant cross-border transactions.

Creating a Network Effect for Accessibility: Ripple's approach to partnerships creates a network effect that enhances accessibility to cross-border financial services. As more financial institutions join the network, the benefits of collaboration and interoperability multiply. This network effect contributes to the creation of a more accessible and inclusive global financial system, breaking down barriers to entry for businesses and individuals.

Conclusion: Nurturing Collaboration for a Cohesive Future:

Partnerships between different payment systems are essential for overcoming the challenges of interoperability in cross-border payments. Ripple's innovative solutions, driven by the Interledger Protocol, offer a transformative pathway to foster collaboration and coordination among diverse systems. By providing a unified framework, Ripple contributes to a future where cross-border transactions are not only efficient and cost-effective but also accessible to a broader global audience. As we progress through subsequent chapters, we will further explore how Ripple's approach aligns with its broader mission of transforming the landscape of international transactions and fostering global financial inclusion.

Friction going cross-network

In the dynamic landscape of cross-border payments, the challenge of interoperability extends beyond technical integration and partnerships. A significant impediment to achieving seamless connectivity is the friction that arises when transactions move across different networks. This chapter explores the complexities and obstacles introduced by the friction going cross-network, examining the various points of resistance and inefficiencies that hinder the smooth flow of funds. From disparities in protocols to the lack of a standardized framework, we delve into the intricacies of cross-network transactions and how Ripple's innovative solutions, particularly the Interledger Protocol (ILP), strategically address these challenges, aiming to eliminate friction and foster a more cohesive global financial system.

Navigating Friction in Cross-Network Transactions:

Disparities in Protocols and Standards: One of the primary sources of friction in cross-network transactions stems from the disparities in protocols and standards employed by different payment networks. Each network may have its own set of rules, formats, and communication protocols, leading to friction when funds need to traverse from one network to another. The lack of a universal standard complicates the interoperability of diverse systems.

Incompatibility of Ledger Technologies: Friction is amplified by the incompatibility of ledger technologies used by different networks. Various payment systems operate on distinct ledger infrastructures, such as blockchain or traditional databases. The inability of these ledgers to seamlessly communicate and reconcile transactions introduces inefficiencies and delays when funds move across networks.

Complexities in Transaction Settlement: Settling transactions across networks introduces complexities due to differences in settlement mechanisms. Some networks may employ real-time settlement, while others may follow a batch processing model. The mismatch in settlement processes can lead to delays, creating friction and uncertainty in the cross-network transaction journey.

Socio-Economic Impact of Cross-Network Friction:

Operational Inefficiencies and Delays: Friction in cross-network transactions results in operational inefficiencies and delays. The complexities introduced by varying protocols and ledger technologies require additional time and resources for financial institutions to navigate. This operational overhead not only delays transaction processing but also increases the overall costs associated with cross-border payments.

Increased Costs Passed to End-Users: The costs incurred in overcoming friction when going cross-network are often passed on to end-users. Financial institutions may need to invest in specialized infrastructure and resources to manage the complexities of cross-network transactions. These increased operational costs are reflected in the fees charged for cross-border payment services, impacting the affordability of such transactions for businesses and individuals.

Uncertainty in Transaction Status: The lack of a standardized framework for cross-network transactions introduces uncertainty in transaction status. As funds move through different networks, the varied settlement processes and reconciliation mechanisms make it challenging to provide real-time visibility into transaction progress. This lack of transparency creates uncertainty for both financial institutions and end-users.

Ripple's Approach to Eliminating Cross-Network Friction:

Interledger Protocol (ILP) as a Unifying Layer: Ripple's innovative approach to eliminating friction in cross-network transactions is centered around the Interledger Protocol (ILP). ILP serves as a unifying layer that transcends the disparities in protocols, ledger technologies, and settlement mechanisms. By providing a standardized framework for communication and value exchange, ILP aims to streamline cross-network transactions and mitigate the challenges introduced by friction.

Standardized Communication for Seamless Transactions: ILP introduces standardized communication for seamless transactions across networks. The protocol establishes a common language that enables different payment systems to communicate effectively. This standardized communication ensures that transaction information is accurately interpreted and processed, reducing the complexities associated with varying protocols and standards.

Interoperability Across Diverse Ledger Technologies: Ripple's ILP facilitates interoperability across diverse ledger technologies. Whether a payment system operates on a blockchain or traditional database, ILP provides a bridge that allows funds to move seamlessly. The compatibility with various ledger technologies eliminates one of the major sources of friction in cross-network transactions, fostering a more interconnected financial ecosystem.

Empowering Global Financial Inclusion:

Efficient and Cost-Effective Cross-Border Transactions: Ripple's focus on eliminating cross-network friction contributes to more efficient and cost-effective cross-border transactions. By providing a standardized layer with ILP, financial institutions can streamline their operations and reduce the time and resources required to navigate different networks. This efficiency translates into cost savings, allowing for more affordable cross-border payment services.

Real-Time Visibility for Enhanced Transparency: ILP enhances transparency in cross-network transactions by providing real-time visibility into transaction progress. Financial institutions and end-users can track the status of funds as they move across networks, reducing uncertainty and enhancing the overall transparency of cross-border payments. This real-time visibility is crucial for building trust and confidence in the financial system.

Accessible Cross-Border Financial Services: Eliminating friction in cross-network transactions aligns with Ripple's mission of fostering global financial inclusion. The efficiency and affordability achieved through ILP make cross-border financial services more accessible to a broader audience. Businesses and individuals in regions that were previously underserved can now participate in the global economy, contributing to greater financial inclusion.

Conclusion: Streamlining the Cross-Network Journey with ILP:

Friction in cross-network transactions poses significant challenges to the efficiency and accessibility of cross-border payments. Ripple's innovative solutions, driven by the Interledger Protocol, offer a transformative pathway to eliminate this friction. By providing a standardized layer that transcends disparities in protocols, ledger technologies, and settlement processes, ILP contributes to a future where cross-network transactions are seamless, efficient, and accessible to businesses and individuals around the world. As we progress through subsequent chapters, we will further explore how Ripple's approach aligns with its broader mission of transforming the landscape of international transactions and fostering global financial inclusion.

Chapter 7: The Call for Modernization
Current landscape untenable long-term

The relentless pace of technological advancement has ushered in an era of unprecedented connectivity and accessibility. In the realm of cross-border payments, the call for modernization echoes louder than ever. This chapter explores the imperative for transforming the current landscape, emphasizing that the existing systems are untenable in the long term. From the limitations of legacy infrastructure to the demands of a globalized digital economy, we delve into the intricacies that render the status quo unsustainable. Additionally, we will examine how Ripple's innovative solutions, particularly the use of the XRP Ledger and Interledger Protocol (ILP), align with the broader call for modernization and offer a transformative vision for the future of cross-border payments.

Unraveling the Limitations of Legacy Infrastructure:

Inefficiencies of Traditional Banking Systems: The current landscape of cross-border payments is dominated by traditional banking systems that rely on outdated infrastructure. These systems, developed in a pre-digital era, are marked by inefficiencies, manual processes, and legacy technologies that struggle to meet the demands of the modern global economy. The inefficiencies of traditional banking systems contribute to delays, high costs, and a lack of transparency in cross-border transactions.

Limited Transaction Speed and Accessibility: Legacy infrastructure imposes limitations on transaction speed and accessibility. The reliance on batch processing and correspondent banking models introduces delays in transaction processing, especially for international transfers. Additionally, the fragmented nature of traditional systems limits accessibility, hindering the seamless flow of funds across borders and creating disparities in financial services availability.

Challenges in Regulatory Compliance: Traditional banking systems grapple with the challenges of regulatory compliance in an increasingly complex global regulatory landscape. The patchwork of regulations across different jurisdictions poses difficulties for financial institutions in ensuring compliance with diverse legal frameworks. This complexity contributes to operational inefficiencies and adds layers of friction to cross-border transactions.

The Digital Economy's Demand for Innovation:

Rising Expectations in a Digital Era: The advent of the digital economy has raised expectations for faster, more transparent, and cost-effective cross-border payments. In a world where information travels at the speed of light, the sluggish pace of traditional systems becomes a bottleneck for businesses and individuals. The demand for instant transactions, real-time visibility, and reduced costs is a driving force behind the call for modernization.

Emergence of Fintech Disruptors: Fintech disruptors have emerged as agile and innovative players challenging the status quo of traditional banking systems. These disruptors leverage cutting-edge technologies to offer solutions that address the shortcomings of legacy infrastructure. The rise of digital-native financial services highlights the need for traditional systems to evolve and adapt to the changing landscape of cross-border payments.

Increasing Complexity of Global Transactions: As global transactions become more intricate and interconnected, the limitations of traditional systems become more pronounced. The demand for cross-border transactions involves not only financial institutions but also a diverse array of stakeholders, including technology providers, regulators, and end-users. Navigating this complexity requires a modernized approach that can seamlessly integrate and coordinate across diverse networks.

Ripple's Vision for Modernizing Cross-Border Payments:

Utilizing the XRP Ledger for Speed and Efficiency: Ripple's vision for modernization is anchored in the utilization of the XRP Ledger, a decentralized blockchain technology. The XRP Ledger enables fast and efficient cross-border transactions by providing a secure and scalable infrastructure. The use of XRP as a bridge currency facilitates real-time settlement, eliminating the delays associated with traditional batch processing models.

Interledger Protocol (ILP) for Seamless Interoperability: Ripple's commitment to modernization extends to the use of the Interledger Protocol (ILP), which serves as a unifying framework for different payment networks. ILP enables seamless interoperability by establishing a common language for communication and value exchange. The protocol's design allows disparate systems to collaborate effortlessly, overcoming the limitations of incompatible protocols and standards.

Addressing Liquidity Challenges: Ripple's approach to modernization includes addressing the liquidity challenges inherent in traditional cross-border payment systems. The use of XRP as a bridge currency eliminates the need for pre-funded nostro accounts, freeing up capital that can be deployed more efficiently. This reduction in liquidity constraints contributes to cost savings and enhances the overall efficiency of cross-border transactions.

Empowering Financial Inclusion Through Modernization:

Extending Financial Services to the Unbanked: Modernizing cross-border payments aligns with Ripple's mission of fostering financial inclusion. By leveraging innovative technologies, Ripple's solutions create opportunities to extend financial services to the unbanked and underbanked populations. The efficiency and accessibility introduced through modernization contribute to breaking down barriers and enabling broader participation in the global economy.

Reducing Costs for Businesses and Individuals: The modernization of cross-border payments through Ripple's solutions translates into cost reduction for businesses and individuals. The elimination of inefficiencies, delays, and unnecessary intermediaries lowers the overall operational costs associated with international transactions. These cost savings contribute to making cross-border payments more affordable and accessible.

Enhancing Accessibility in Emerging Markets: Modernization has a direct impact on enhancing accessibility, especially in emerging markets. Ripple's solutions, by leveraging the XRP Ledger and ILP, provide a pathway for financial institutions in these markets to connect seamlessly with the global financial system. The reduced friction in cross-border transactions opens up opportunities for small businesses, individuals, and entire economies to participate more actively in international trade and finance.

Conclusion: Ripple's Role in the Modernization Imperative:

The call for modernization in cross-border payments is a response to the challenges posed by legacy infrastructure in an era of rapid technological evolution. Ripple's innovative solutions, driven by the XRP Ledger and Interledger Protocol, play a pivotal role in addressing these challenges. By modernizing the infrastructure, streamlining transaction processes, and fostering financial inclusion, Ripple contributes to a future where cross-border payments are efficient, accessible, and aligned with the demands of the global digital economy. As we progress through the concluding sections, we will further explore the broader implications of modernization and the transformative impact it can have on the international financial landscape.

Incumbents slow to evolve systems

In the ever-evolving landscape of cross-border payments, the inertia of incumbents poses a significant obstacle to progress. This section delves into the challenges associated with traditional institutions slow to evolve their systems. From the complexities of legacy infrastructure to the resistance against change, we explore the factors contributing to the sluggish pace of adaptation within established financial entities. Additionally, we examine how Ripple's forward-thinking approach, driven by the XRP Ledger and Interledger Protocol, addresses these challenges and paves the way for a more agile and modernized cross-border payment ecosystem.

The Struggle of Traditional Financial Institutions:

Legacy Systems and Institutional Inertia: Traditional financial institutions are often encumbered by legacy systems that have been in place for decades. These systems, built on outdated technologies, struggle to keep pace with the demands of the digital era. The sheer complexity of these legacy systems, combined with the fear of disrupting established processes, creates a significant barrier to innovation and modernization.

Risk Aversion and Compliance Concerns: The financial industry is inherently risk-averse, driven by the need for stability and security. This risk aversion extends to the adoption of new technologies and operational models. Traditional financial institutions, bound by stringent regulatory requirements, often hesitate to embrace innovative solutions due to concerns about compliance, data security, and the potential for operational disruptions.

Resistance to Change in Organizational Culture: Institutional adaptation is not only a technological challenge but also a cultural one. The entrenched organizational cultures within traditional financial institutions can resist change, particularly when it involves a fundamental shift in operational paradigms. The hierarchical structures, established workflows, and resistance to disruption can impede the agility required for swift adaptation.

The Slow Evolution of Cross-Border Payment Systems:

Inefficiencies Perpetuated by Established Systems: The persistence of legacy systems perpetuates inefficiencies in cross-border payment processes. Traditional systems, designed for a different era, rely on manual processes, batch-oriented transaction models, and correspondent banking networks. These inefficiencies result in delays, high costs, and a lack of transparency in cross-border transactions, hindering the evolution of the payment ecosystem.

Complex Interconnectedness of Global Financial Networks: The global financial ecosystem is intricately interconnected, with established systems serving as integral components. The complex web of relationships between financial institutions, payment networks, and intermediaries creates challenges for seamless integration of new technologies. The slow evolution of interconnected networks contributes to the persistence of friction in cross-border payments.

Fragmentation and Lack of Standardization: Fragmentation and a lack of standardization further impede the evolution of cross-border payment systems. Different regions, currencies, and financial institutions operate with varying protocols and standards. The absence of a standardized framework hinders interoperability and the seamless exchange of value across diverse systems, perpetuating the fragmented nature of the current landscape.

Ripple's Approach to Overcoming Institutional Inertia:

Utilizing XRP Ledger for Rapid Settlement: Ripple's approach to overcoming institutional inertia is rooted in the utilization of the XRP Ledger. The XRP Ledger's decentralized and efficient blockchain technology facilitates rapid settlement of cross-border transactions. By providing a secure and scalable infrastructure, XRP Ledger addresses the limitations of traditional settlement processes, offering a compelling alternative to the slow settlement mechanisms of legacy systems.

Interledger Protocol (ILP) as a Unifying Framework: Ripple tackles the challenges posed by institutional inertia through the use of the Interledger Protocol (ILP). ILP serves as a unifying framework that transcends the disparities in protocols and standards. This standardized communication protocol allows disparate systems to communicate seamlessly, fostering interoperability and reducing the resistance caused by incompatible technologies and operational models.

Addressing Liquidity Challenges for Institutional Buy-In: Ripple's strategic approach involves addressing liquidity challenges, a key concern for institutional buy-in. By using XRP as a bridge currency, Ripple eliminates the need for pre-funded nostro accounts. This reduction in liquidity constraints not only enhances the efficiency of cross-border transactions but also presents a compelling proposition for traditional financial institutions seeking cost savings and operational optimization.

Empowering Traditional Institutions Through Collaboration:

Collaborative Partnerships with Financial Institutions: Rather than positioning itself as a disruptor, Ripple advocates for collaborative partnerships with traditional financial institutions. By working hand-in-hand with incumbents, Ripple aims to facilitate a gradual transition towards modernized cross-border payment systems. This collaborative approach acknowledges the existing strengths and market presence of established institutions while offering innovative solutions to enhance their operational efficiency.

Gradual Integration to Ensure Smooth Transition: Ripple recognizes the need for a gradual integration approach to ensure a smooth transition for traditional financial institutions. The phased implementation of Ripple's solutions allows incumbents to adopt new technologies without disrupting existing operations. This approach minimizes the perceived risks associated with abrupt changes and provides a pathway for institutions to evolve at their own pace.

Supporting Compliance Through Regulatory Engagement: Acknowledging the regulatory concerns of traditional financial institutions, Ripple actively engages with regulators to address compliance challenges. By fostering open communication and collaboration with regulatory bodies, Ripple aims to create a regulatory environment that supports the adoption of innovative technologies. This proactive engagement contributes to building trust and confidence in the regulatory compliance of Ripple's solutions.

Conclusion: Ripple's Role in Accelerating Evolution:

In the face of institutional inertia, Ripple stands as a catalyst for accelerating the evolution of cross-border payment systems. By strategically leveraging the XRP Ledger, Interledger Protocol, and collaborative partnerships with traditional financial institutions, Ripple addresses the challenges of legacy systems and fosters a more agile and modernized financial ecosystem. As we progress through the subsequent sections, we will further explore the transformative impact of Ripple's approach on the international financial landscape and the broader implications for the future of cross-border payments.

Regulatory push for improvements

In the intricate world of cross-border payments, the role of regulatory frameworks cannot be overstated. This section delves into the regulatory landscape, exploring the imperative for improvements and modernization. From the challenges posed by disparate regulatory environments to the global push for a more cohesive framework, we examine the factors shaping the regulatory landscape. Additionally, we explore how Ripple's innovative solutions, particularly the XRP Ledger and Interledger Protocol (ILP), align with and contribute to the regulatory push for improvements in cross-border payments.

Navigating the Complexity of Cross-Border Payment Regulation:

Disparate Regulatory Environments: One of the fundamental challenges in the cross-border payment landscape is the existence of disparate regulatory environments across jurisdictions. Each country operates with its own set of rules, compliance standards, and reporting requirements. This regulatory fragmentation creates a complex web of legal frameworks that financial institutions must navigate when facilitating cross-border transactions, leading to inefficiencies and compliance challenges.

Cross-Border Compliance Challenges: The cross-border nature of payments introduces unique compliance challenges for financial institutions. Ensuring adherence to diverse regulatory requirements, anti-money laundering (AML) standards, and know your customer (KYC) regulations becomes a complex task. The lack of a standardized approach to cross-border compliance contributes to operational inefficiencies, delays, and increased compliance costs.

Evolution of Regulatory Expectations: Regulatory expectations in the financial industry continue to evolve in response to emerging risks, technological advancements, and global economic shifts. Regulators are increasingly focusing on enhancing transparency, reducing financial crime, and fostering financial inclusion. The evolving regulatory landscape places additional pressure on financial institutions to adapt their cross-border payment systems to meet these changing expectations.

Global Initiatives for Regulatory Cohesion:

International Organizations and Standardization: Recognizing the challenges posed by disparate regulations, international organizations are actively working towards standardization. Bodies such as the Financial Action Task Force (FATF) and the Bank for International Settlements (BIS) play a crucial role in setting global standards for financial regulations. The aim is to create a more cohesive regulatory framework that facilitates cross-border transactions while addressing concerns related to security, transparency, and financial integrity.

Collaboration Between Jurisdictions: Collaboration between jurisdictions has become essential for addressing cross-border regulatory challenges. Bilateral and multilateral agreements facilitate cooperation between regulatory bodies, fostering a more harmonized approach to cross-border payments. The collaborative efforts aim to create an environment where financial institutions can navigate regulatory requirements more seamlessly, promoting efficiency and reducing compliance-related frictions.

Emergence of Regulatory Sandboxes: Some jurisdictions are exploring innovative approaches to regulatory oversight through the establishment of regulatory sandboxes. These sandboxes provide a controlled environment for financial institutions to test new technologies and solutions under the guidance of regulators. The goal is to encourage innovation while ensuring compliance with regulatory standards, contributing to the evolution of cross-border payment systems.

Ripple's Alignment with Regulatory Objectives:

Transparent and Compliant Cross-Border Transactions: Ripple's approach to cross-border payments aligns with regulatory objectives by prioritizing transparency and compliance. The XRP Ledger and Interledger Protocol (ILP) provide a secure and transparent infrastructure for cross-border transactions. The decentralized nature of the XRP Ledger ensures immutability and auditability, contributing to the traceability required by regulatory standards.

Addressing Compliance Challenges with ILP: The Interledger Protocol (ILP) serves as a unifying framework that addresses compliance challenges associated with disparate regulations. ILP establishes a standardized communication protocol, allowing different payment networks to communicate effectively. By providing a common language for value exchange, ILP facilitates compliance with diverse regulatory requirements, reducing the complexity of cross-border compliance.

Regulatory Engagement and Collaboration: Ripple actively engages with regulatory bodies to contribute to the ongoing dialogue surrounding cross-border payments. By fostering collaboration with regulators, Ripple seeks to align its solutions with evolving regulatory expectations. Proactive engagement includes providing insights into the capabilities of the XRP Ledger and ILP to address regulatory concerns, contributing to the development of a regulatory environment conducive to innovation.

Empowering Regulatory Compliance Through Technology:

Blockchain Technology and Immutable Records: Blockchain technology, the foundation of the XRP Ledger, offers immutable records that contribute to regulatory compliance. The decentralized and distributed nature of blockchain ensures that transaction records are tamper-resistant and verifiable. This characteristic is crucial for meeting regulatory expectations related to auditability and the prevention of financial crimes.

Smart Contracts for Automated Compliance: Smart contracts, a feature of blockchain technology, can be leveraged to automate certain aspects of regulatory compliance. By embedding compliance rules into smart contracts, financial institutions using Ripple's solutions can automate processes such as identity verification and transaction monitoring. This automation not only enhances efficiency but also reduces the risk of human error in compliance procedures.

Enhancing AML and KYC Processes: Ripple's solutions contribute to enhancing anti-money laundering (AML) and know your customer (KYC) processes. The transparent nature of transactions on the XRP Ledger, combined with the ability to embed compliance rules in smart contracts, facilitates more effective AML and KYC procedures. This contributes to the overall integrity of cross-border transactions and aligns with regulatory expectations.

Conclusion: Ripple's Role in Regulatory Modernization:

The regulatory push for improvements in cross-border payments reflects the global recognition of the need for a more cohesive and transparent financial ecosystem. Ripple's commitment to aligning with regulatory objectives, leveraging innovative technologies, and actively engaging with regulators positions it as a key player in the ongoing modernization of regulatory frameworks. As we delve into subsequent chapters, we will further explore the transformative impact of regulatory improvements on the future of cross-border payments and Ripple's role in shaping this evolution.

Emerging solutions show promise

In the dynamic landscape of cross-border payments, a wave of emerging solutions is reshaping the way we envision global transactions. This section explores the promise held by innovative technologies and approaches that are gaining traction in the pursuit of modernizing cross-border payments. From decentralized finance (DeFi) to central bank digital currencies (CBDCs), we delve into the potential of these emerging solutions and their role in addressing the challenges of the current system. Additionally, we examine how Ripple's innovative use of the XRP Ledger and Interledger Protocol (ILP) aligns with and complements these promising developments.

Decentralized Finance (DeFi) and Cross-Border Transactions:

The Rise of Decentralized Finance: Decentralized Finance, or DeFi, has emerged as a transformative force in the financial industry. Built on blockchain technology, DeFi platforms aim to recreate traditional financial services in a decentralized and permissionless manner. The principles of transparency, accessibility, and efficiency inherent in DeFi align with the goals of modernizing cross-border payments.

Smart Contracts and Automated Transactions: DeFi leverages smart contracts, self-executing contracts with the terms of the agreement directly written into code. This technology enables the creation of automated financial instruments and transactions, reducing the need for intermediaries and streamlining processes. In the context of cross-border payments, smart contracts can facilitate quicker, more transparent, and cost-effective transactions.

Challenges and Opportunities in DeFi for Cross-Border Payments: While DeFi holds promise, it also faces challenges such as scalability, regulatory compliance, and user adoption. The potential for decentralized cross-border payments lies in overcoming these challenges, providing a more inclusive financial system where individuals and businesses can transact globally without the traditional hurdles associated with cross-border transfers.

Central Bank Digital Currencies (CBDCs) and Cross-Border Integration:

Introduction of Central Bank Digital Currencies: Central Bank Digital Currencies (CBDCs) represent a digital form of a country's national currency issued and regulated by the central bank. The development and exploration of CBDCs by central banks worldwide aim to modernize financial systems, enhance payment efficiency, and address the challenges of cross-border transactions.

Potential Impact on Cross-Border Payments: CBDCs have the potential to significantly impact cross-border payments by offering a digital alternative to traditional fiat currencies. The ability to transact in digital currencies issued and regulated by central banks could streamline cross-border transactions, reducing settlement times, minimizing costs, and enhancing transparency.

Challenges in CBDC Implementation: The implementation of CBDCs presents challenges related to interoperability, privacy, and international coordination. Harmonizing different CBDCs to enable seamless cross-border transactions requires collaboration between central banks and regulatory bodies. Overcoming these challenges is crucial for realizing the full potential of CBDCs in the context of cross-border payments.

Blockchain Interoperability and the Interledger Protocol (ILP):

Interoperability Challenges in Blockchain Networks: The blockchain ecosystem is characterized by a multitude of networks, each with its own protocols and standards. Achieving interoperability—seamless communication and value transfer between disparate blockchains—remains a significant challenge. Interoperability is essential for creating a cohesive global financial infrastructure and unlocking the full potential of blockchain technology.

Interledger Protocol (ILP) as a Unifying Framework: The Interledger Protocol (ILP), championed by Ripple, addresses the challenge of interoperability in cross-border payments. ILP serves as a unifying framework that enables different payment networks, ledgers, and blockchains to communicate and transact seamlessly. By providing a common language for value exchange, ILP fosters interoperability, reducing friction in cross-border transactions.

The Role of ILP in Enhancing Emerging Solutions: ILP plays a crucial role in enhancing the potential of emerging solutions, such as DeFi and CBDCs. By providing a standardized protocol for communication, ILP facilitates the integration of different financial systems and ensures compatibility between emerging solutions. This interoperability is essential for creating a cohesive and accessible global financial network.

Ripple's Synergy with Emerging Solutions:

XRP Ledger as a Bridge Currency: Ripple's innovative use of the XRP Ledger positions it as a key player in the realm of emerging solutions. The XRP Ledger, with its decentralized and scalable architecture, serves as a bridge currency for cross-border transactions. The use of XRP as a bridge asset enables real-time settlement, reducing the reliance on pre-funded nostro accounts and minimizing liquidity challenges.

Complementing DeFi Principles: Ripple's approach aligns with the principles of DeFi by leveraging blockchain technology for transparency, accessibility, and efficiency. The XRP Ledger's ability to support smart contracts and enable automated transactions complements the goals of DeFi, offering a decentralized alternative for cross-border payments.

Facilitating CBDC Integration: Ripple's solutions, particularly the XRP Ledger and ILP, can facilitate the integration of CBDCs into the broader cross-border payment landscape. By providing interoperability and a standardized protocol for communication, Ripple contributes to the creation of a seamless and efficient environment where CBDCs can coexist and transact with other digital assets.

Conclusion: Converging Paths Toward a Modernized Future:

As we witness the rise of DeFi, the exploration of CBDCs, and the pursuit of blockchain interoperability, the future of cross-border payments is taking shape. These emerging solutions show promise in addressing the pain points of the current system and paving the way for a more modernized, transparent, and inclusive financial ecosystem. Ripple's strategic use of the XRP Ledger and ILP positions it at the intersection of these converging paths, contributing to the evolution of cross-border payments into a more efficient and interconnected global network. In the subsequent chapters, we will further explore the transformative potential of these emerging solutions and their collective impact on the future of international transactions.

Conclusion
Recapping the pain points

In the dynamic landscape of cross-border payments, the call for modernization resounds as a collective response to the pain points inherent in the current system. As we conclude our exploration, it is essential to recapitulate the significant pain points that have spurred the quest for transformative solutions, particularly focusing on Ripple's vision with the XRP Ledger.

Recapping the Pain Points: Unveiling the Fractured Landscape

Limited Speed of International Transfers: The speed of international transfers has long been a contentious issue, with stark disparities between domestic and global transaction times. The cumbersome nature of batch processing and the reliance on a slow correspondent banking model have perpetuated delays that impact individuals and businesses alike. The inefficiencies in the current system have highlighted the pressing need for expeditious cross-border transactions to meet the demands of a globalized economy.

Exorbitant Cost of Cross-Border Payments: Costs associated with cross-border payments have proven to be a significant deterrent for businesses and individuals seeking to engage in global transactions. The imposition of expensive fees, coupled with wide foreign exchange spreads and a lack of fee transparency, has contributed to the high expense of cross-border transactions. As we recapture these pain points, it becomes evident that reducing costs is fundamental to fostering broader use cases for cross-border payments.

Challenges in Access to Cross-Border Systems: While technology has advanced at an unprecedented pace, a significant portion of the global population remains unbanked. Emerging markets face friction in accessing cross-border systems, and small businesses encounter barriers that impede their participation in international trade. The complexity of existing systems further alienates individuals, emphasizing the critical need for inclusive solutions that bridge the gap in access to cross-border financial services.

Opacity Plaguing International Transfers: The opacity surrounding international transfers has been a longstanding concern, characterized by limited transparency into the status of transactions. Tracking payments across diverse chains remains challenging, contributing to errors and mismatches that can have severe consequences for beneficiaries. In our exploration of the pain points, addressing the opacity in cross-border transactions emerges as a pivotal factor in enhancing the reliability and efficiency of global payment systems.

Demand for Liquidity and Mitigating Volatility: Volatility in currency markets and the reliance on pre-funded nostro accounts present liquidity challenges that escalate the costs of cross-border transactions. The captured capital in these pre-funded accounts could be deployed more effectively to drive economic growth. Recognizing the need for liquidity solutions is crucial to establishing a financial ecosystem that is not only efficient but also resilient to the fluctuations inherent in global currency markets.

Interoperability Struggles in Cross-Border Systems: The current landscape is fraught with interoperability challenges arising from disconnected payment silos and a lack of standardization. Cross-network transactions face friction due to the absence of seamless communication between diverse systems. Partnerships become imperative, yet the absence of standardized protocols hinders the fluid exchange of value. As we summarize these pain points, the call for interoperability becomes an integral component of the roadmap toward a modernized cross-border payment ecosystem.

The Untenable Nature of the Current Landscape: Perhaps the overarching pain point is the untenable nature of the current cross-border payment landscape. Incumbents, slow to evolve, perpetuate inefficiencies, and regulatory frameworks struggle to keep pace with technological advancements. The urgency for modernization is driven by the recognition that the existing system is unsustainable in the face of rapid digitization and the evolving needs of a globalized world.

Ripple's Vision: A Catalyst for Change

As we recapture these pain points, it becomes evident that Ripple's vision with the XRP Ledger is positioned as a catalyst for change in the cross-border payments paradigm. By strategically addressing these pain points, Ripple aims to usher in a new era characterized by speed, cost-efficiency, accessibility, transparency, and interoperability.

Speeding Up Transactions with XRP Ledger: Ripple addresses the limited speed of international transfers by leveraging the XRP Ledger, providing a decentralized and efficient blockchain infrastructure for rapid settlement. The use of XRP as a bridge currency facilitates real-time settlement, significantly reducing the time required for cross-border transactions.

Cost-Efficiency through Liquidity Solutions: Ripple's approach tackles the exorbitant costs associated with cross-border payments by addressing liquidity challenges. Through the elimination of pre-funded nostro accounts and the deployment of XRP as a bridge currency, Ripple's solutions contribute to cost-efficiency, offering a compelling proposition for businesses and individuals alike.

Enhanced Access and Financial Inclusion: Recognizing the challenges in access to cross-border systems, Ripple advocates for a more inclusive financial ecosystem. By streamlining transaction processes and reducing friction, Ripple's solutions empower small businesses, individuals, and unbanked populations to participate more actively in the global economy.

Transparency and Accountability: Ripple's vision aligns with the imperative of transparency in international transactions. The decentralized nature of the XRP Ledger ensures immutability and accountability, addressing the opacity plaguing current cross-border systems. By providing a clear and auditable record of transactions, Ripple contributes to the reliability and trustworthiness of global payments.

Interoperability as a Core Tenet: Interoperability is at the core of Ripple's vision, with the Interledger Protocol (ILP) serving as a unifying framework. ILP enables seamless communication between disparate systems, overcoming the interoperability struggles present in the current landscape. Ripple's commitment to partnerships and collaborative efforts further reinforces the drive toward a more interconnected cross-border payment ecosystem.

Adaptive Solutions for a Modern Era: In response to the untenable nature of the current landscape, Ripple stands as a proponent of adaptive solutions. Through strategic engagement with regulators, collaboration with traditional financial institutions, and the gradual integration of innovative technologies, Ripple aims to modernize cross-border payments without causing disruptive shocks to the existing financial infrastructure.

Transitioning to the Next Generation: The Imperative for Change

In conclusion, the pain points embedded in the current cross-border payment ecosystem serve as a clarion call for change. Ripple's vision, anchored in the transformative capabilities of the XRP Ledger and Interledger Protocol, positions it as a harbinger of this change. As we transition to the next generation of cross-border payments, it is imperative to recognize that the journey involves not just overcoming challenges but fundamentally reimagining the way value is exchanged on a global scale.

The case for change is not merely a response to the inadequacies of the present but a proactive pursuit of a future where cross-border transactions are seamless, efficient, and accessible to all. The intersection of technological innovation, regulatory evolution, and collaborative efforts marks the convergence of paths toward a modernized era of cross-border payments. Ripple's role in this transition underscores its commitment to shaping a financial landscape that is responsive to the needs of a digital age.

As we embark on this journey toward a next-generation cross-border payment ecosystem, the lessons learned from the pain points of the past serve as guiding beacons. The imperative for change is not just a narrative of challenges; it is a narrative of possibilities, opportunities, and the promise of a more interconnected and inclusive global financial system. The concluding chapters of this book will delve into the broader implications of this transition, exploring the transformative impact on international finance and the role of Ripple's innovative solutions in shaping the future of cross-border payments.

The case for change

In the rapidly evolving landscape of cross-border payments, the imperative for change resonates as a guiding principle that propels the industry toward a future marked by efficiency, transparency, and inclusivity. As we navigate the complex terrain of financial transactions across borders, it becomes essential to construct a compelling case for change, understanding the challenges inherent in the current system and articulating a vision for a more responsive, resilient, and innovative paradigm. In this concluding chapter, we delve into the multifaceted aspects of the case for change, exploring the economic, technological, and societal imperatives that underscore the need for a transformative overhaul in cross-border payments.

Economic Imperatives: Rethinking Global Financial Flows

The economic imperatives for change in cross-border payments are rooted in the recognition that the existing system imposes substantial costs and inefficiencies on businesses, financial institutions, and individuals engaged in international transactions.

Cost Reduction and Increased Efficiency: One of the primary economic drivers for change lies in the pursuit of cost reduction and increased efficiency. The current cross-border payment landscape is characterized by exorbitant fees, wide foreign exchange spreads, and the operational burden of maintaining pre-funded nostro accounts. These factors contribute to high transaction costs and protracted settlement times, inhibiting the smooth flow of capital across borders. By streamlining processes, reducing reliance on intermediary banks, and leveraging innovative technologies, the case for change revolves around creating a more cost-effective and efficient global financial infrastructure.

Unlocking Economic Potential: The economic imperatives for change extend beyond mere cost reduction. A revamped cross-border payment system has the potential to unlock economic opportunities by fostering greater financial inclusion and enabling small businesses in emerging markets to participate more actively in global trade. The efficient movement of funds across borders can stimulate economic growth, empower entrepreneurs, and contribute to the overall prosperity of nations. The case for change, therefore, is intricately linked to the broader goal of harnessing the economic potential of a more interconnected and accessible global financial ecosystem.

Technological Imperatives: Embracing Innovation for Seamless Transactions

Technological imperatives form a cornerstone of the case for change in cross-border payments, driven by the swift evolution of digital technologies that offer innovative solutions to longstanding challenges.

Blockchain and Distributed Ledger Technology (DLT): The emergence of blockchain and distributed ledger technology has been a transformative force in reimagining cross-border payments. These technologies provide a decentralized and secure framework for transactions, eliminating the need for traditional intermediaries and introducing transparency into the payment process. Blockchain's ability to facilitate real-time settlement and create tamper-resistant transaction records aligns with the technological imperatives for change, offering a robust foundation for a modernized cross-border payment system.

Smart Contracts and Automation: Smart contracts, embedded within blockchain technology, introduce automation into cross-border transactions. The programmable nature of smart contracts allows for the automatic execution of predefined conditions, reducing the reliance on manual processes and minimizing the risk of errors. Automation not only accelerates transaction times but also enhances the overall efficiency and reliability of cross-border payments. The case for change is intricately tied to the integration of smart contract capabilities, paving the way for a more streamlined and technologically advanced payment ecosystem.

Interoperability as a Catalyst: Interoperability, or the seamless integration of diverse payment networks, is a critical technological imperative for change. The current fragmented landscape, characterized by disconnected payment silos and the absence of standardized communication protocols, introduces friction into cross-border transactions. The case for change emphasizes the importance of interoperability, with solutions like the Interledger Protocol (ILP) acting as a catalyst for connecting disparate systems. By fostering interoperability, the technological imperatives for change aim to create a more interconnected and accessible global financial network.

Societal Imperatives: Driving Financial Inclusion and Accessibility

Beyond economic and technological considerations, the case for change in cross-border payments is grounded in societal imperatives that advocate for financial inclusion, accessibility, and fairness.

Empowering the Unbanked: A significant societal imperative for change lies in the quest for financial inclusion. Despite technological advancements, a substantial portion of the global population remains unbanked, lacking access to basic financial services. The case for change recognizes the potential of innovative solutions, such as those offered by Ripple's XRP Ledger, to empower the unbanked by providing them with the means to engage in cross-border transactions. The decentralized nature of blockchain technology, combined with the accessibility of digital assets, has the potential to bridge the financial inclusion gap, extending the benefits of a connected global economy to previously underserved populations.

Ensuring Fair and Transparent Transactions: Societal imperatives also underscore the need for fairness and transparency in cross-border transactions. The opacity plaguing the current system, with limited visibility into transaction statuses and complex fee structures, has implications for individuals and businesses alike. The case for change advocates for a more transparent and accountable financial ecosystem, where the terms of transactions are clear, fees are disclosed, and participants can engage with confidence. The transformative impact of blockchain and distributed ledger technology in promoting transparency aligns with these societal imperatives, fostering a sense of trust in cross-border payments.

Regulatory Imperatives: Navigating a Shifting Landscape

The regulatory imperatives for change in cross-border payments reflect the evolving nature of the global regulatory landscape, with policymakers recognizing the need to adapt to technological advancements and address the shortcomings of the current system.

Modernizing Regulatory Frameworks: The pace of technological innovation has outstripped the capabilities of existing regulatory frameworks, leading to a call for their modernization. The case for change acknowledges that regulators need to adapt to the changing dynamics of cross-border payments, leveraging technology to enhance oversight, mitigate risks, and ensure compliance with evolving standards. Collaborative efforts between the private sector, including innovative fintech solutions like Ripple, and regulatory bodies are crucial for establishing a regulatory framework that fosters innovation while safeguarding the integrity of the financial system.

Fostering Innovation and Competition: Regulatory imperatives for change extend beyond compliance to fostering innovation and competition. Recognizing that the concentration of power within traditional financial institutions can stifle innovation and limit consumer choices, regulators are increasingly advocating for an environment that encourages competition and rewards technological advancements. The case for change aligns with these regulatory imperatives, positioning innovative solutions like Ripple's XRP Ledger as catalysts for fostering healthy competition and driving positive changes in the cross-border payment landscape.

Ripple's Contribution to the Case for Change: Aligning Vision with Imperatives

In the context of the broader case for change, Ripple's vision with the XRP Ledger emerges as a strategic alignment with economic, technological, societal, and regulatory imperatives. Ripple's commitment to addressing the pain points of the current system aligns with the economic imperative of reducing costs, unlocking economic potential, and fostering greater efficiency in cross-border transactions.

Technologically, Ripple's use of the XRP Ledger and the Interledger Protocol responds to the imperatives of embracing blockchain innovation, integrating smart contract capabilities, and promoting interoperability. By providing a decentralized and transparent framework, Ripple contributes to societal imperatives of financial inclusion, transparency, and fairness in cross-border payments.

Ripple's engagement with regulators and its commitment to compliance align with the regulatory imperatives of modernizing frameworks, fostering innovation, and ensuring a level playing field. Ripple's collaborative approach, evidenced by ongoing partnerships and dialogue with regulatory bodies, positions it as a key participant in shaping the regulatory landscape for cross-border payments.

The Collaborative Path Forward: Uniting Stakeholders for Transformation

As we conclude our exploration of the case for change in cross-border payments, it is evident that the journey toward a modernized and inclusive system requires collaboration among diverse stakeholders. Financial institutions, technology innovators, regulatory bodies, and the broader global community must unite in a concerted effort to drive transformation.

Collaboration as the Cornerstone: The case for change underscores the importance of collaboration as the cornerstone of transformative initiatives. Financial institutions, traditionally seen as competitors, must recognize the shared interest in creating a more efficient and accessible global financial ecosystem. Collaboration between the public and private sectors is essential, with regulators playing a pivotal role in providing guidance, ensuring compliance, and fostering an environment that encourages innovation.

The Ripple Effect of Innovative Solutions: Innovative solutions, exemplified by Ripple's vision with the XRP Ledger, have the potential to create a ripple effect across the industry. By demonstrating the viability of blockchain technology, introducing efficient settlement mechanisms, and promoting transparency, these solutions set a precedent for the broader adoption of transformative technologies in cross-border payments. The case for change is not merely a theoretical proposition but a tangible reality embodied in the tangible impacts of innovative solutions.

Looking Ahead: Navigating the Roadmap of Transformation

As we navigate the roadmap of transformation in cross-border payments, the case for change serves as a guiding compass, directing our attention toward the destination of a more connected, efficient, and inclusive global financial system. The economic, technological, societal, and regulatory imperatives provide a comprehensive framework for understanding the multifaceted nature of the challenges and opportunities that lie ahead.

The collaborative efforts of stakeholders, coupled with the innovative solutions offered by forward-thinking companies like Ripple, lay the foundation for a future where cross-border payments are characterized by speed, efficiency, transparency, and accessibility. The case for change invites us to embrace the possibilities inherent in transformative initiatives, recognizing that the journey toward a modernized cross-border payment ecosystem is not just a technological evolution but a societal and economic revolution.

In the chapters that precede this conclusion, we have explored the pain points of the current system, analyzed the transformative potential of emerging solutions, and delved into Ripple's strategic vision with the XRP Ledger. As we look ahead, the case for change challenges us to be proactive architects of a future where financial transactions transcend borders seamlessly, empowering individuals, stimulating economic growth, and fostering a more interconnected world.

Transitioning to the next generation

As we stand on the precipice of transformative change in the realm of cross-border payments, the imperative to transition to the next generation is palpable. This concluding chapter marks not just the end of a journey through the intricacies of the current system's pain points and the potential solutions offered by Ripple's XRP Ledger, but the beginning of a new era defined by innovation, efficiency, and inclusivity. The narrative of transitioning to the next generation encapsulates the multifaceted nature of this evolution, weaving together technological advancements, economic considerations, and societal aspirations into a tapestry that envisions a future where cross-border payments cease to be a bottleneck and become a conduit for global prosperity.

Redefining Cross-Border Dynamics: A Vision for Tomorrow

The transition to the next generation signifies a departure from the limitations and inefficiencies of the existing cross-border payment paradigm. It is a collective acknowledgment that the evolving needs of a globalized world demand a financial infrastructure capable of seamlessly facilitating transactions across borders. This redefinition goes beyond mere technological upgrades; it encompasses a fundamental shift in mindset, where cross-border payments are viewed not as obstacles but as enablers of economic growth, financial inclusion, and global collaboration.

Technological Renaissance: The Role of Blockchain and Beyond

At the heart of the transition to the next generation lies a technological renaissance that reshapes the very foundations of cross-border payments. Blockchain technology, with its decentralized and tamper-resistant architecture, emerges as a linchpin in this transformation. The distributed ledger, epitomized by Ripple's XRP Ledger, introduces a level of transparency, security, and efficiency previously unseen in traditional systems.

Decentralization and Trust: Decentralization is the keystone of the technological shift, challenging the centralized models that have historically governed cross-border transactions. By distributing transactional authority across a network of nodes, blockchain technology instills trust in a system where trust was often compromised. The immutable nature of the ledger ensures a transparent and auditable record of transactions, fostering a sense of confidence among participants.

Smart Contracts and Automation: Smart contracts, a manifestation of programmable code embedded within blockchain platforms, play a pivotal role in automating cross-border transactions. These self-executing contracts streamline processes, reduce the risk of errors, and accelerate settlement times. The transition to smart contracts signifies a departure from manual, time-consuming procedures to an era of automated, near-instantaneous transactions.

Interoperability as the Bridge: Interoperability emerges as the bridge connecting disparate systems in the transition to the next generation. The Interledger Protocol (ILP), championed by Ripple, serves as a unifying force that transcends the siloed nature of existing payment networks. The ability of different systems to seamlessly communicate and transact with each other becomes a cornerstone, dismantling barriers and fostering a more interconnected global financial ecosystem.

Economic Realignment: Navigating Cost Efficiency and Financial Inclusion

A critical facet of transitioning to the next generation revolves around an economic realignment that seeks to make cross-border transactions not only cost-efficient but also inclusive and accessible to all.

Cost-Efficiency Through XRP Ledger: The economic underpinnings of this transition hinge on the inherent cost-efficiency offered by blockchain platforms, particularly the XRP Ledger. Ripple's strategic use of XRP as a bridge currency addresses the historical challenges associated with pre-funded nostro accounts, liberating trapped capital and reducing the costs incurred by financial institutions. The transition to a model where XRP serves as a liquidity bridge holds the promise of significantly diminishing the expenses associated with cross-border transactions.

Financial Inclusion at the Forefront: The transition to the next generation places financial inclusion at the forefront of its objectives. Ripple's commitment to leveraging blockchain for financial inclusion aligns with the broader aspiration of extending access to cross-border financial services to the unbanked and underbanked populations. The decentralized and borderless nature of blockchain technology opens doors for individuals who were previously excluded from participating in the global economy.

Empowering Small Businesses: In the evolving landscape, small businesses emerge as key beneficiaries of the transition. The reduction in transaction costs, streamlined processes, and increased accessibility to global markets empower small enterprises to engage in cross-border trade with greater ease. The next generation envisions a scenario where the barriers that once impeded the growth of small businesses are dismantled, fostering a more equitable global economic landscape.

Societal Impact: Paving the Way for Transparency and Trust

The societal impact of transitioning to the next generation is profound, paving the way for a financial ecosystem characterized by transparency, trust, and empowerment.

Transparent Transactions: One of the fundamental shifts in the societal dimension is the advent of transparent transactions. The current opacity plaguing cross-border payments, where participants often lack visibility into the status and details of transactions, gives way to a system where every transaction is recorded on an immutable ledger. The transparent nature of blockchain ensures that all stakeholders have real-time access to the details of transactions, mitigating disputes and fostering trust.

Empowering Individuals: The transition to the next generation is about empowering individuals, granting them greater control over their financial interactions. Blockchain's decentralized nature ensures that individuals have direct ownership and control over their assets, reducing reliance on intermediaries. The advent of user-centric financial solutions, facilitated by blockchain platforms, enables individuals to participate more actively in the global financial system.

Trust in the Digital Age: Trust, a cornerstone of any financial system, undergoes a renaissance in the digital age. Blockchain's ability to create tamper-resistant records and smart contracts that execute predefined conditions engenders a sense of trust among participants. The shift from centralized authority to decentralized consensus mechanisms transforms the narrative of trust, making it intrinsic to the architecture of the system rather than dependent on external assurances.

Regulatory Dynamics: Navigating the Balancing Act

The transition to the next generation necessitates a recalibration of regulatory dynamics to strike a delicate balance between fostering innovation and safeguarding the integrity of the financial system.

Adaptive Regulatory Frameworks: Regulatory frameworks must adapt to the rapid evolution of technology. The transition to the next generation requires regulators to adopt an adaptive stance, engaging with innovative solutions to understand their implications and iteratively updating frameworks to accommodate technological advancements. The collaborative dialogue between regulators and innovators becomes imperative to strike the right balance.

Ensuring Compliance and Security: Security and compliance remain paramount concerns in the transition. Regulators play a pivotal role in ensuring that new technologies adhere to established standards, safeguarding against illicit activities, and protecting the interests of participants. The integration of robust compliance mechanisms within blockchain platforms, coupled with transparent audit trails, addresses regulatory concerns and enhances the security of cross-border transactions.

Fostering Innovation: Regulatory bodies are increasingly recognizing the need to foster innovation within the financial sector. The transition to the next generation involves a collaborative effort between regulators and innovators to create an environment that encourages experimentation, rewards technological advancements, and ensures that regulatory frameworks do not stifle the potential benefits of new technologies.

Ripple's Role in Facilitating the Transition: A Strategic Vision

Ripple, through its strategic vision anchored in the XRP Ledger and Interledger Protocol, plays a pivotal role in facilitating the transition to the next generation of cross-border payments. The alignment of Ripple's objectives with the overarching goals of cost efficiency, financial inclusion, transparency, and regulatory compliance positions it as a catalyst for industry-wide transformation.

Ripple's Contribution to Cost Efficiency: Ripple's utilization of XRP as a bridge currency addresses the cost inefficiencies embedded in traditional cross-border payment models. The XRP Ledger's ability to facilitate rapid, low-cost transactions positions it as a cost-effective alternative to the current system, providing financial institutions with a tool to optimize liquidity management and reduce operational costs.

Ripple's Commitment to Financial Inclusion: Ripple's commitment to financial inclusion aligns with the societal imperative of empowering individuals globally. By leveraging blockchain technology, Ripple aims to extend the benefits of cross-border financial services to the unbanked and underbanked populations. The transition to the next generation, as facilitated by Ripple, envisions a more inclusive financial ecosystem that transcends geographical and socio-economic boundaries.

Ripple's Role in Promoting Transparency: Transparency lies at the core of Ripple's strategic vision. The XRP Ledger's transparent and immutable nature ensures that all transactions are recorded in a tamper-resistant manner, addressing the pain points associated with limited visibility into transaction statuses. Ripple's efforts to promote transparency align with the societal imperative of fostering trust and accountability in cross-border transactions.

Ripple's Collaboration with Regulators: Ripple's engagement with regulators exemplifies its commitment to navigating the evolving regulatory landscape. By actively collaborating with regulatory bodies, Ripple seeks to contribute to the development of adaptive frameworks that balance the need for innovation with the imperative of maintaining a secure and compliant financial ecosystem. Ripple's role in fostering constructive dialogue between the private sector and regulators positions it as a key participant in shaping the regulatory dynamics of the next generation.

Challenges on the Path to the Next Generation: Navigating Complexity

While the transition to the next generation holds immense promise, it is not devoid of challenges. Navigating the complexity inherent in this transformative journey requires a nuanced understanding of the hurdles that may impede progress.

Integration Challenges: The integration of blockchain technology into existing financial infrastructures poses a significant challenge. Financial institutions, accustomed to legacy systems, may encounter resistance to change and face the daunting task of seamlessly integrating blockchain solutions. The transition necessitates a careful balance between preserving the stability of existing systems and embracing the innovation offered by blockchain.

Regulatory Uncertainty: The regulatory landscape remains a source of uncertainty. The lack of standardized regulatory frameworks for blockchain and digital assets introduces complexity and ambiguity. Navigating diverse regulatory approaches across jurisdictions requires a concerted effort to establish common standards that promote innovation while addressing regulatory concerns. The challenge lies in striking a harmonious balance that fosters global interoperability.

Technological Maturation: The maturation of blockchain technology is an ongoing process. While blockchain has demonstrated its potential, ongoing advancements and refinements are essential to address scalability issues, enhance security, and optimize performance. The challenge is to ensure that the technology matures at a pace that aligns with the industry's expectations and requirements.

Collaboration as the Catalyst: Uniting Stakeholders for Success

As we navigate the challenges and complexities inherent in transitioning to the next generation of cross-border payments, collaboration emerges as the catalyst for success. The involvement of diverse stakeholders—financial institutions, technology providers, regulatory bodies, and the global community—is essential to overcome hurdles and collectively shape the future of cross-border transactions.

Financial Institutions as Champions of Change: Financial institutions play a pivotal role as champions of change. Their proactive engagement in embracing innovative solutions, such as those offered by Ripple, is critical to catalyzing the transition. Collaboration among financial institutions to establish interoperability and streamline processes is key to unlocking the full potential of the next generation.

Regulators as Facilitators of Innovation: Regulators, by adopting a facilitative role, can expedite the transition to the next generation. Collaborative efforts between regulators and the private sector, exemplified by ongoing dialogues initiated by Ripple, can lead to the development of regulatory frameworks that strike a balance between fostering innovation and safeguarding the integrity of the financial system.

Technology Providers as Innovators: Technology providers, including blockchain innovators like Ripple, are at the forefront of driving innovation. Their commitment to developing scalable, secure, and interoperable solutions is pivotal for the successful transition. Collaboration between technology providers and financial institutions ensures that solutions are not only technologically robust but also align with the practical requirements of the industry.

Global Community as Advocates of Inclusivity: The global community, including end-users and individuals, has a role to play in advocating for inclusivity and accessibility. By embracing the benefits of the next generation of cross-border payments, individuals can contribute to a groundswell of support that reinforces the societal imperatives underpinning the transition.

Charting the Course for a Connected Future

As we conclude this exploration into the transition to the next generation of cross-border payments, the overarching narrative is one of optimism, innovation, and collaborative effort. The challenges ahead are met with a collective determination to overcome hurdles and build a financial ecosystem that transcends boundaries, fosters economic growth, and empowers individuals globally.

The roadmap to the next generation is not a linear path but a dynamic, iterative process. It requires continuous collaboration, adaptability, and a shared vision among stakeholders. The technological, economic, societal, and regulatory dimensions are interwoven, requiring a holistic approach that navigates complexity while embracing the transformative potential of emerging technologies.

In the chapters leading to this conclusion, we explored the pain points of the current cross-border payment system, delved into the innovative solutions presented by Ripple's XRP Ledger, and articulated the imperatives for change. Now, as we stand at the threshold of the next generation, the call to action is clear: to collaborate, innovate, and collectively shape a future where cross-border payments are seamless, efficient, and inclusive.

The transition to the next generation is not just a technological evolution but a testament to the collective will of stakeholders to redefine the way we transact globally. As we chart the course for a connected future, let us embark on this journey with a shared commitment to building a cross-border payment ecosystem that reflects the ideals of transparency, accessibility, and efficiency—a future where financial transactions transcend borders, connecting individuals and businesses in a global tapestry of prosperity.

THE END

Glossary

Here are some key terms and definitions related to AI-driven cryptocurrency investing:

1. Cross-Border Payments: Financial transactions that involve the transfer of money or assets between individuals, businesses, or financial institutions across different countries.

2. Ripple: A technology company that aims to transform cross-border payments using blockchain and digital assets, with XRP as a key component.

3. XRP Ledger: A decentralized blockchain ledger that facilitates fast and cost-effective cross-border transactions using the XRP digital asset.

4. International Transfers: Movement of funds or assets across borders, often involving different currencies and financial systems.

5. Batch Processing: The practice of grouping multiple transactions together for simultaneous processing, causing delays in cross-border payments.

6. Correspondent Banking Model: A system where banks rely on intermediaries (correspondent banks) to facilitate cross-border transactions, leading to delays and higher costs.

7. Nostro Accounts: Bank accounts held by financial institutions in foreign countries to facilitate international transactions, requiring pre-funded capital.

8. Foreign Exchange Spreads: The difference between the buying and selling rates of currencies, representing the cost of exchanging one currency for another.

9. Transparency: The degree to which information about the status and details of cross-border transactions is easily accessible and understandable.

10. Financial Inclusion: The effort to provide individuals, particularly the unbanked and underbanked, with access to financial services and cross-border payment systems.

11. Blockchain Technology: A decentralized and distributed ledger technology that underlies cryptocurrencies, ensuring transparency, security, and immutability of transactions.

12. Interoperability: The ability of different cross-border payment systems to seamlessly communicate and transact with each other.

13. Regulatory Frameworks: Established rules and regulations set by governments and financial authorities to govern cross-border payments and ensure compliance.

14. Smart Contracts: Self-executing contracts with coded terms and conditions, automating aspects of cross-border transactions and reducing the risk of errors.

15. Decentralization: Distribution of transactional authority across a network, reducing reliance on central authorities and enhancing trust in cross-border payments.

16. Financial Institutions: Organizations such as banks and credit unions that provide financial services, including facilitating cross-border transactions.

17. Innovation: The introduction of new and improved methods, technologies, or processes to enhance the efficiency and effectiveness of cross-border payments.

18. Global Economy: The interconnected system of economies around the world, influenced by cross-border transactions and international trade.

19. Liquidity: The availability of liquid assets, such as XRP, to facilitate smooth and efficient cross-border transactions.

20. Emerging Markets: Developing economies with growing financial sectors that may face challenges in accessing cross-border payment systems.

Potential References

In addition to the content presented in this book, we have compiled a list of supplementary materials that can provide further insights and information on the topics covered. These resources include books, articles, websites, and other materials that were used as references throughout the writing process. We encourage you to explore these materials to deepen your understanding and continue your learning journey. Below is a list of the supplementary materials organized by chapter/topic for your convenience.

Introduction:

World Bank. (2021). "Migration and Remittances Data." Retrieved from https://www.worldbank.org/en/topic/migrationremittancesdiasporaissues/brief/migration-remittances-data

Ripple. (2021). "About Us." Retrieved from https://ripple.com/company/

Chapter 1: Speed of International Transfers:

McKinsey & Company. (2016). "Crossing borders: How online marketplaces can help SMEs grow internationally." Retrieved from https://www.mckinsey.com/business-functions/mckinsey-digital/our-insights/crossing-borders-how-online-marketplaces-can-help-smes-grow-internationally

Federal Reserve. (2020). "The Continued Evolution of Faster Payments in the United States." Retrieved from https://www.federalreserve.gov/paymentsystems/faster-payments-overview.htm

Chapter 2: Cost of Cross-Border Payments:

Bank for International Settlements (BIS). (2020). "Cross-Border Retail Payments." Retrieved from https://www.bis.org/cpmi/publ/d200.htm

European Central Bank. (2019). "Understanding the impact of cross-border instant payments." Retrieved from https://www.ecb.europa.eu/pub/pdf/other/understandingimpactcrossborderinstantpayments201902en.pdf

Chapter 3: Access to Cross-Border Systems:

World Bank. (2019). "Global Findex Database 2017: Measuring Financial Inclusion and the Fintech Revolution." Retrieved from https://globalfindex.worldbank.org/

Financial Stability Board. (2018). "Financial Stability Implications from FinTech." Retrieved from https://www.fsb.org/wp-content/uploads/P110618-1.pdf

Chapter 4: The Opacity of International Transfers:

Financial Action Task Force (FATF). (2020). "Guidance for a Risk-Based Approach to Virtual Assets and Virtual Asset Service Providers." Retrieved from https://www.fatf-gafi.org/publications/fatfrecommendations/documents/guidance-rba-virtual-assets.html

Swift. (2019). "Improving Cross-Border Payments: Building a Platform for Innovation." Retrieved from https://www.swift.com/news-events/press-releases/swift-at-sibos-2019

Chapter 5: The Need for Liquidity:

Reserve Bank of Australia. (2020). "Nostro Reconciliation in the New Payments Platform Environment." Retrieved from https://www.rba.gov.au/payments-and-infrastructure/npp/npp-nostro-reconciliation.html

International Monetary Fund (IMF). (2018). "Cross-Border Payment Services: Innovation and Challenges in Cross-Border Payments." Retrieved from https://www.imf.org/en/Publications/fintech-notes/Issues/2018/09/14/Cross-Border-Payment-Services-Innovation-and-Challenges-in-Cross-Border-Payments-46232

Chapter 6: The Interoperability Challenge:

World Economic Forum. (2020). "Central Bank Digital Currency Policy-Maker Toolkit." Retrieved from http://www3.weforum.org/docs/WEF_CBDC_Policymaker_Toolkit.pdf

Interledger Protocol (ILP). (2021). "About ILP." Retrieved from https://interledger.org/

Chapter 7: The Call for Modernization:

Financial Stability Oversight Council (FSOC). (2018). "Nonbank Financials, Fintech, and Innovation." Retrieved from https://home.treasury.gov/system/files/261/FSOC%20Nonbank%20Report%20-%20July%202018.pdf

Bank of England. (2021). "Future of Finance: Review on the Outlook for the UK Financial System." Retrieved from https://www.bankofengland.co.uk/paper/2021/future-of-finance-review-on-the-outlook-for-the-uk-financial-system

Conclusion:

Financial Stability Board (FSB). (2017). "Financial Stability Implications from FinTech: Supervisory and Regulatory Issues that Merit Authorities' Attention." Retrieved from https://www.fsb.org/wp-content/uploads/R270617-1.pdf

G20. (2019). "G20 Insights for the Digital Era." Retrieved from https://www.g20-insights.org/wp-content/uploads/2019/04/5-10-G20-Insights-for-the-Digital-Era.pdf